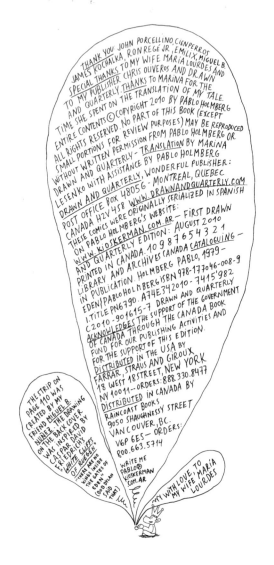

THANK YOU: JOHN PORCELLINO, CIENPERROS JAMES KOCHALKA, RON REGÉ JR., EMILIX, MIGUEL B. SPECIAL THANKS TO MY WIFE MARÍA LOURDES AND TO MY PUBLISHER CHRIS OLIVEROS AND DRAWN AND QUARTERLY. THANKS TO MARINA FOR THE TIME SHE SPENT ON THE TRANSLATION OF MY TALE.
ENTIRE CONTENTS © COPYRIGHT 2010 BY PABLO HOLMBERG ALL RIGHTS RESERVED. NO PART OF THIS BOOK (EXCEPT SMALL PORTIONS FOR REVIEW PURPOSES) MAY BE REPRODUCED WITHOUT WRITTEN PERMISSION FROM PABLO HOLMBERG OR DRAWN AND QUARTERLY - TRANSLATION BY MARINA LESENKO WITH ASSISTANCE BY PABLO HOLMBERG
DRAWN AND QUARTERLY, WONDERFUL PUBLISHER: POST OFFICE BOX 48056 - MONTREAL, QUEBEC CANADA H2V 4S8 WWW.DRAWNANDQUARTERLY.COM
THESE COMICS WERE ORIGINALLY SERIALIZED IN SPANISH ON PABLO HOLMBERG'S WEBSITE: WWW.KIOSKERMAN.COM.AR - FIRST DRAWN AND QUARTERLY EDITION: AUGUST 2010
10 9 8 7 6 5 4 3 2 1
PRINTED IN CANADA.
LIBRARY AND ARCHIVES CANADA CATALOGUING - IN PUBLICATION. HOLMBERG PABLO, 1979 - EDEN / PABLO HOLMBERG ISBN 978-177046-008-9 1. TITLE PN6790. A74E34 2010 - 741.5'982 C2010-901615-7
DRAWN AND QUARTERLY ACKNOWLEDGES THE SUPPORT OF THE GOVERNMENT OF CANADA THROUGH THE CANADA BOOK FUND FOR OUR PUBLISHING ACTIVITIES AND FOR THE SUPPORT OF THIS EDITION.
DISTRIBUTED IN THE USA BY FARRAR, STRAUS AND GIROUX 18 WEST 18 STREET, NEW YORK NY 10011 -- ORDERS: 888.330.8477
DISTRIBUTED IN CANADA BY RAINCOAST BOOKS 9050 SHAUGHNESSY STREET VANCOUVER, BC. V6P 6E5 - ORDERS: 800.663.5714
THE STRIP ON PAGE 110 WAS CREATED BY MY FRIEND MIGUEL B. NUÑEZ. THE DRAWING ON THE BACK COVER WAS INSPIRED BY CASPAR DAVID FRIEDRICH'S "WHITE CLIFFS OF RUEGEN"
"THERE ARE NO KINGS INSIDE THE GATES OF EDEN" (BOB DYLAN SAID THAT)
WRITE ME PABLO@KIOSKERMAN.COM.AR
WITH LOVE, TO MY WIFE MARÍA LOURDES

PABLO HOLMBERG'S
EDEN

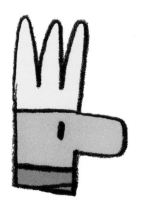

✺ DRAWN & QUARTERLY ✺

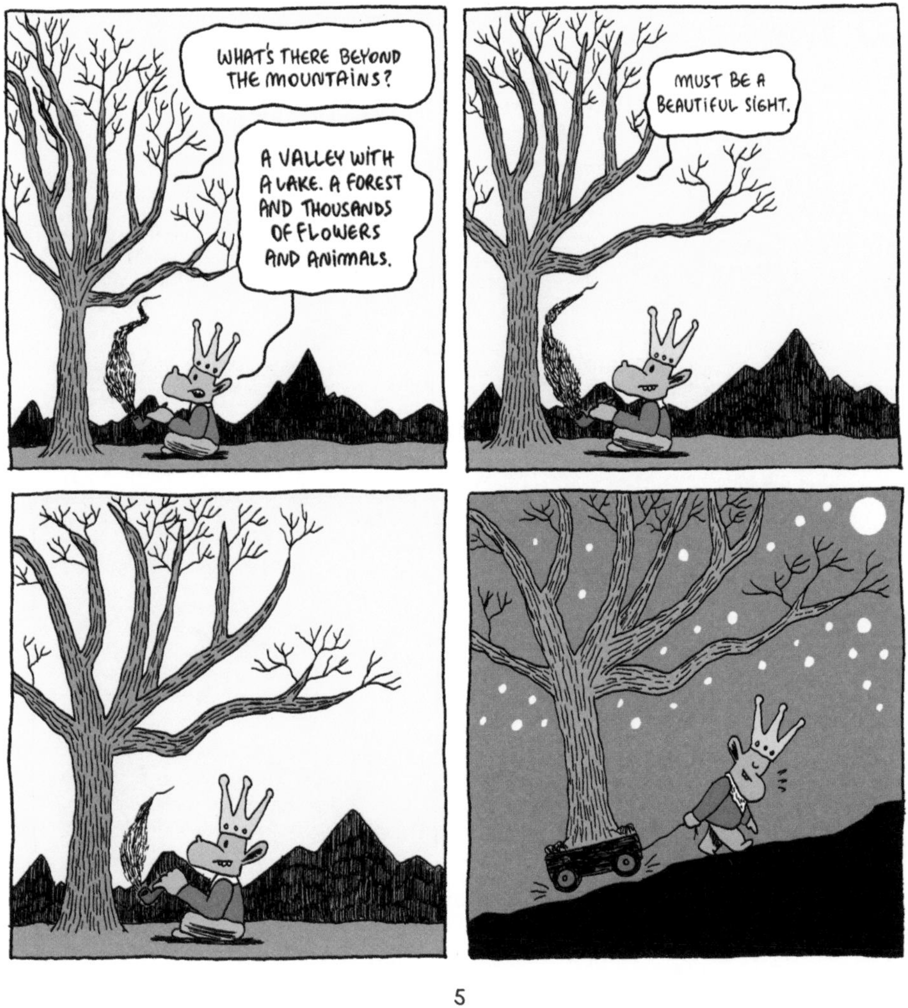
WHAT'S THERE BEYOND THE MOUNTAINS?
A VALLEY WITH A LAKE. A FOREST AND THOUSANDS OF FLOWERS AND ANIMALS.
MUST BE A BEAUTIFUL SIGHT.

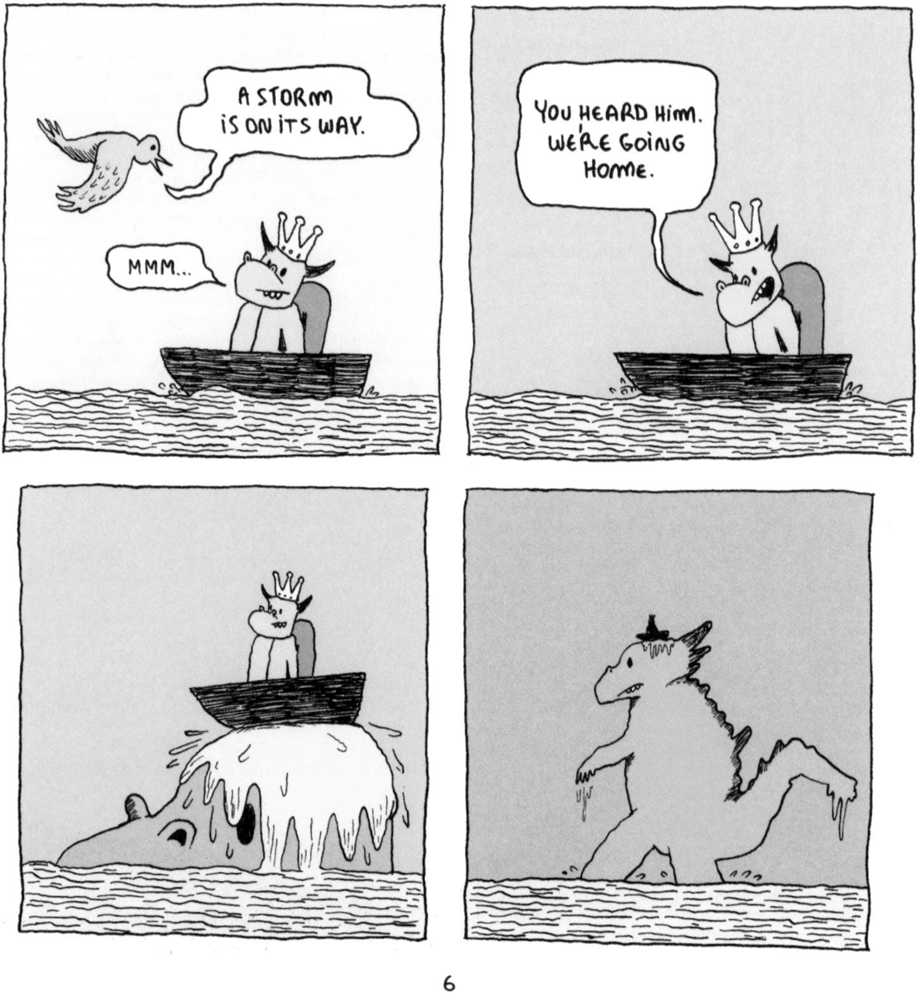
A STORM IS ON ITS WAY.
MMM...
YOU HEARD HIM. WE'RE GOING HOME.

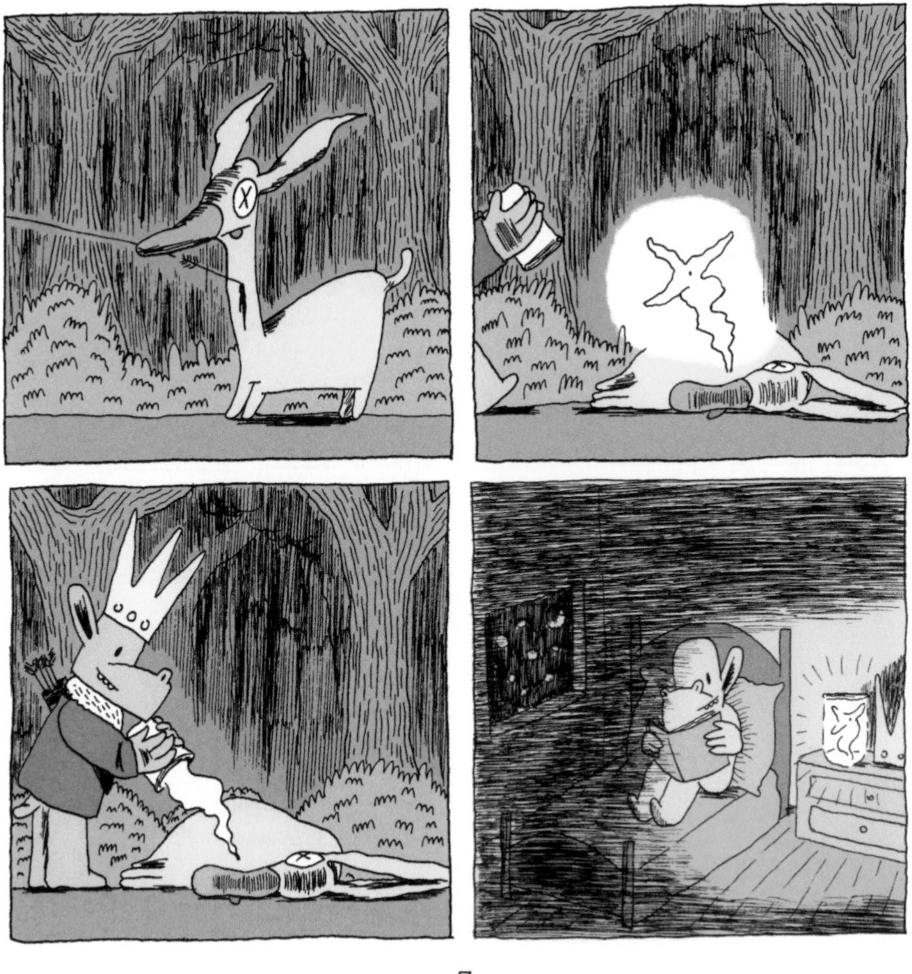

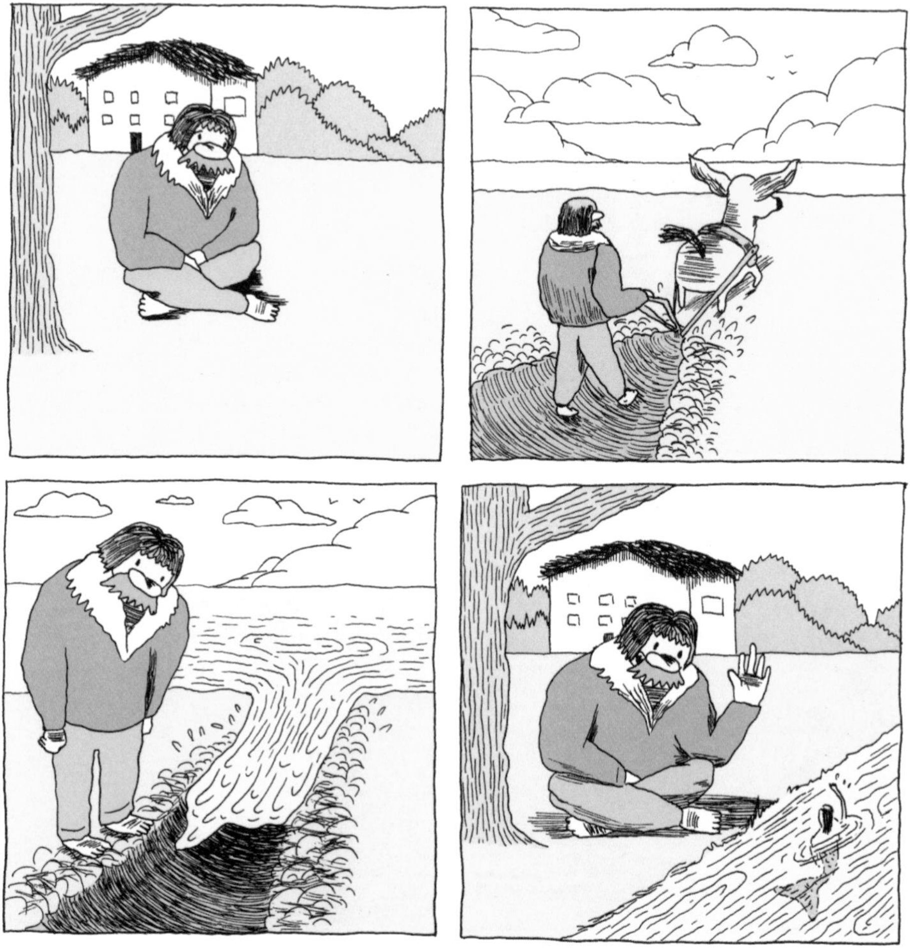

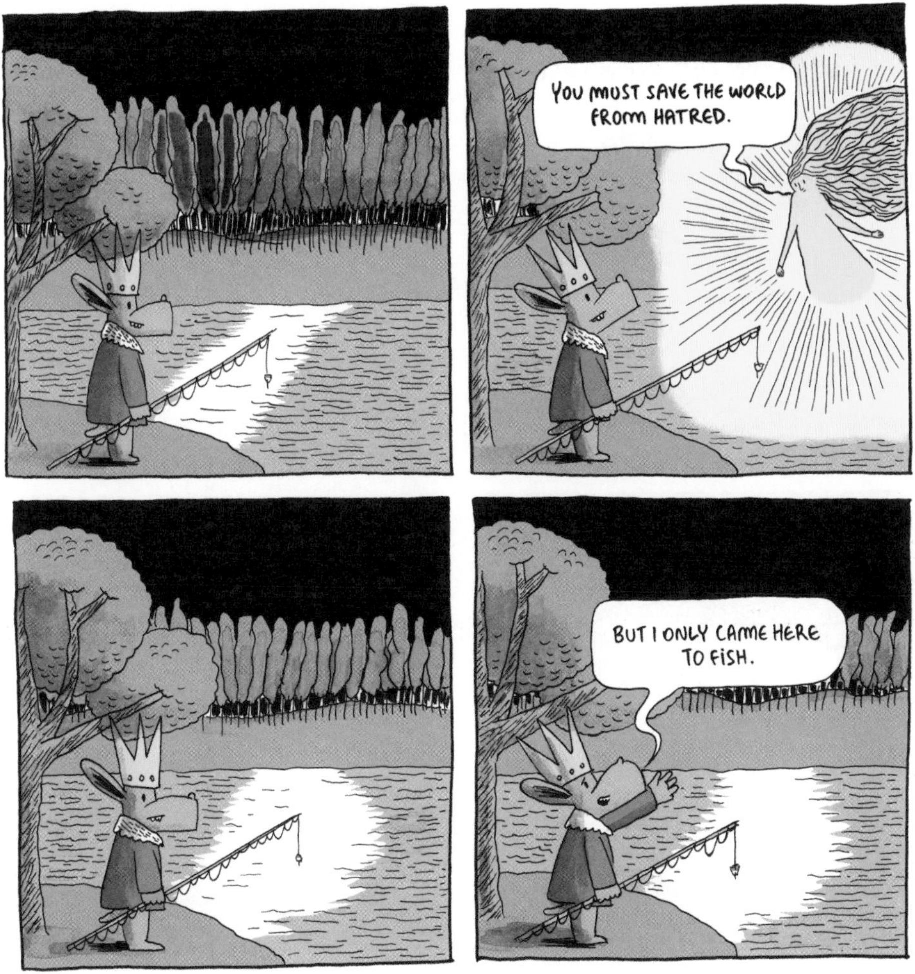
YOU MUST SAVE THE WORLD FROM HATRED.
BUT I ONLY CAME HERE TO FISH.

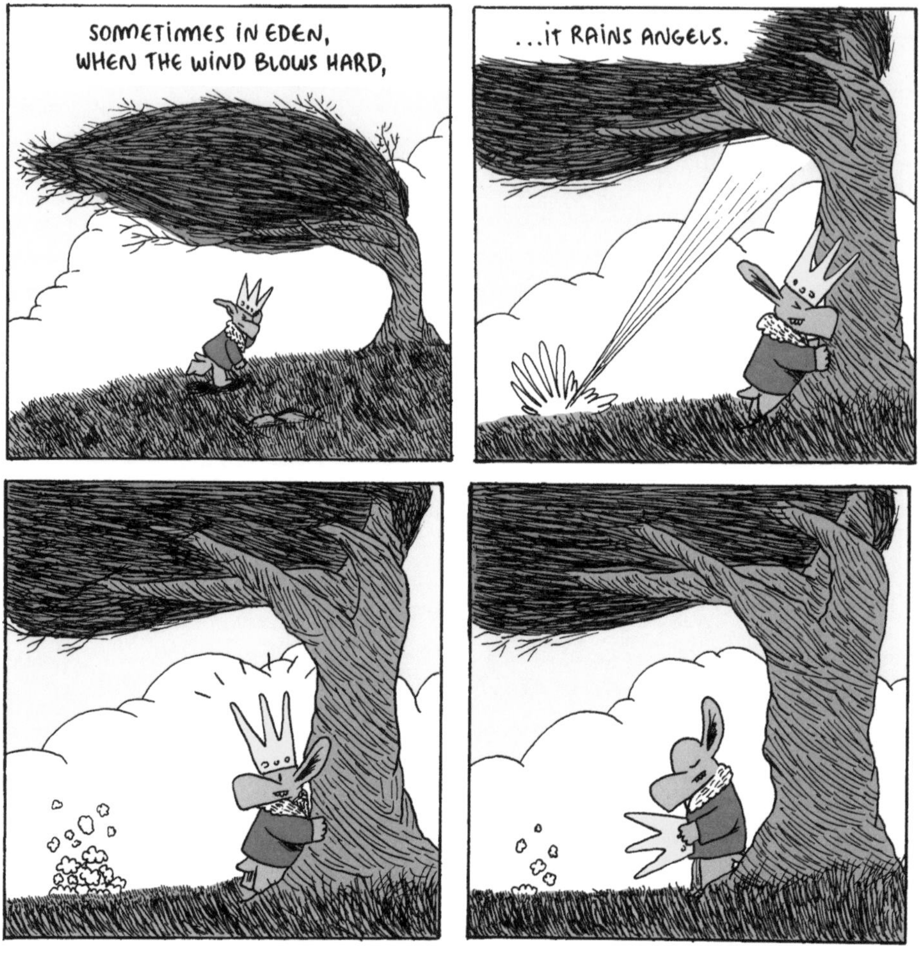
SOMETIMES IN EDEN,
WHEN THE WIND BLOWS HARD,
...IT RAINS ANGELS.

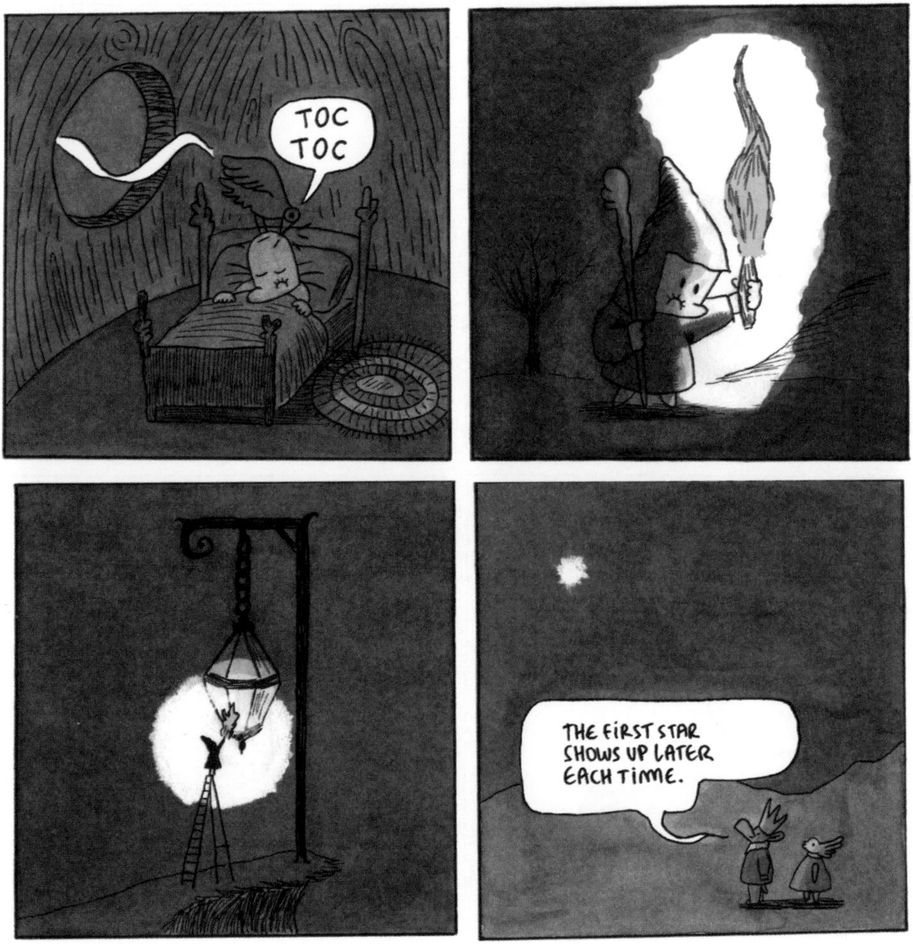
TOC TOC
THE FIRST STAR SHOWS UP LATER EACH TIME.

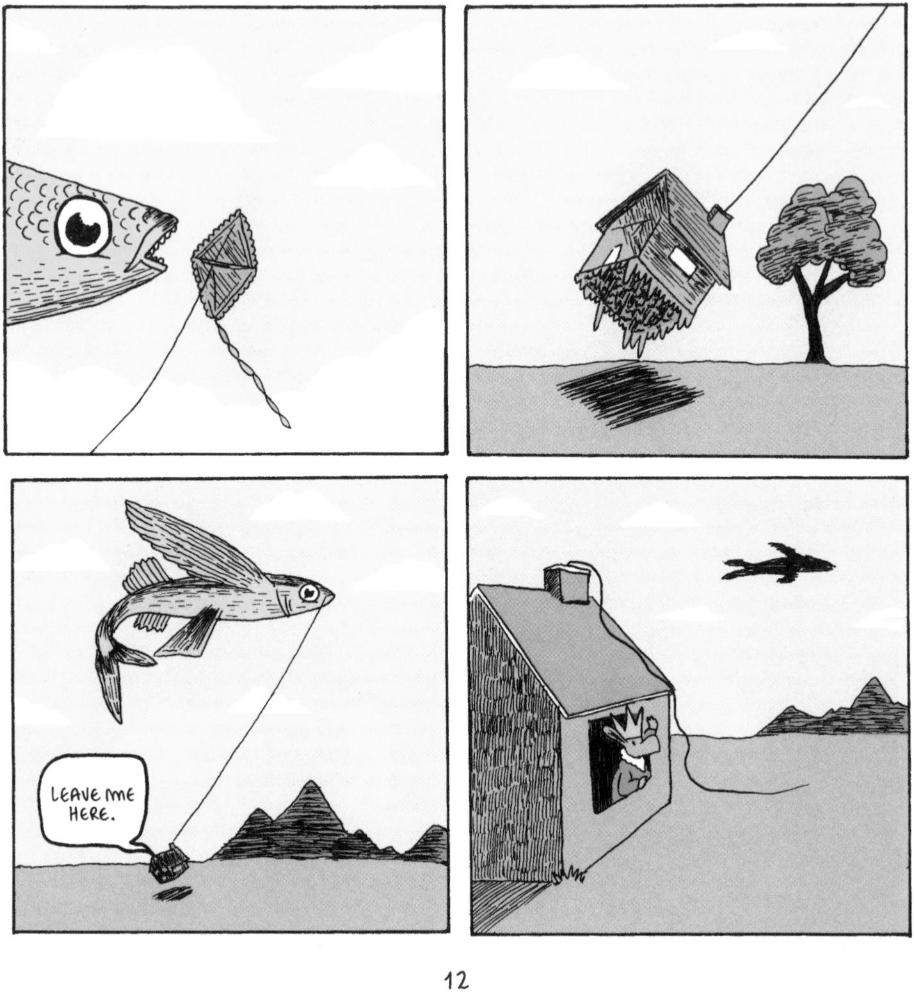
LEAVE ME HERE.

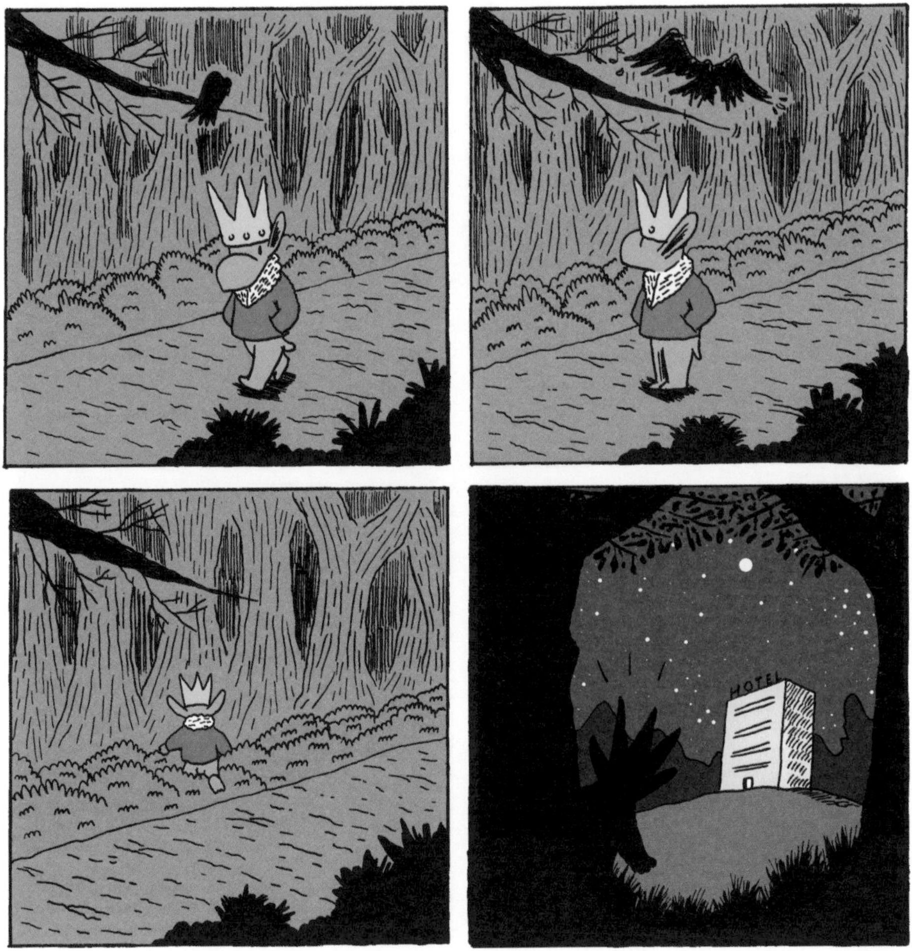
HOTEL

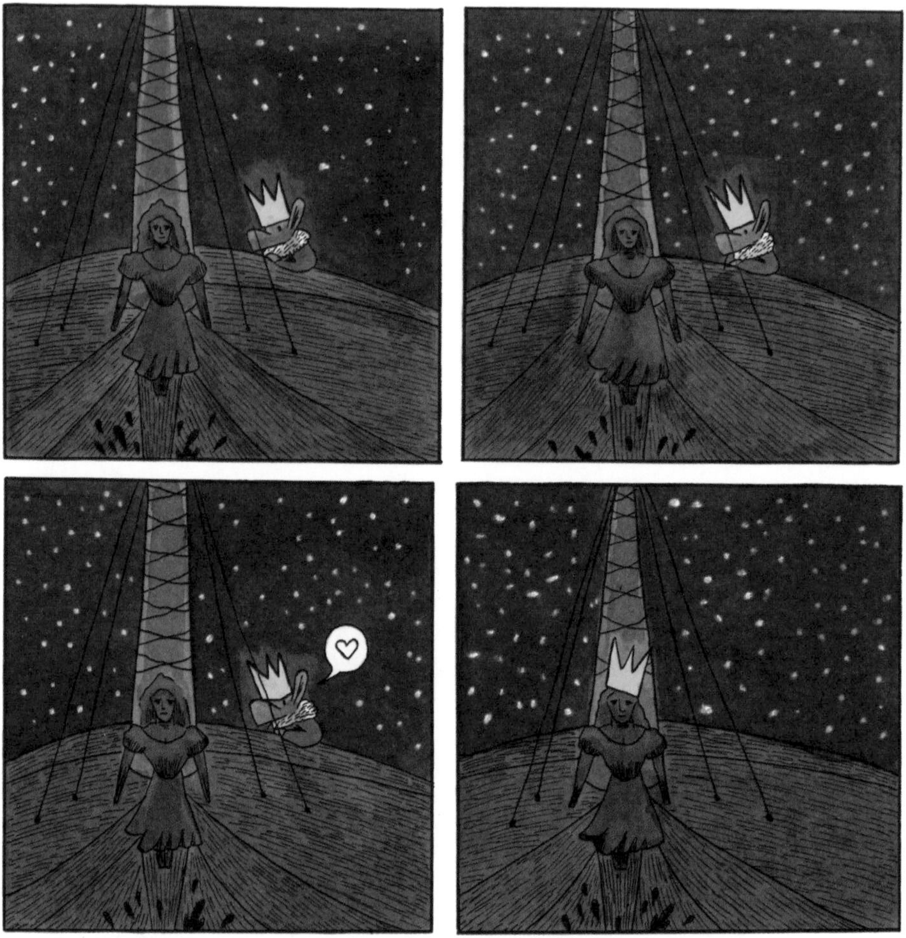

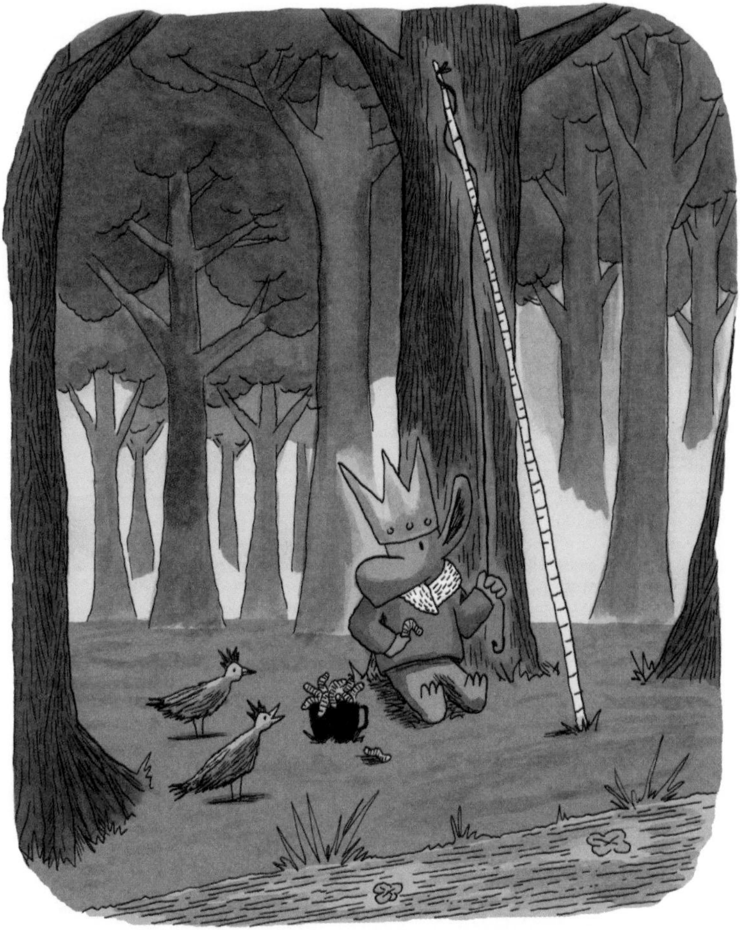

"EXCUSE ME, DO YOU HAVE ANY LEFTOVERS?"

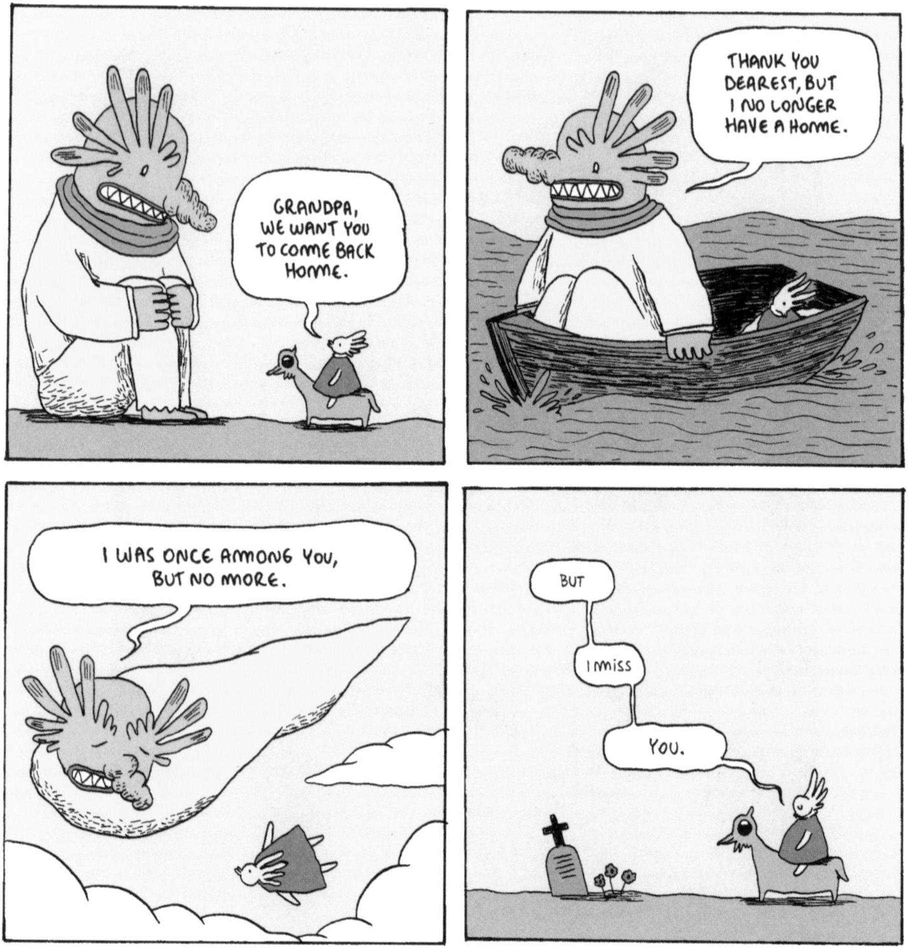
GRANDPA, WE WANT YOU TO COME BACK HOME.
THANK YOU DEAREST, BUT I NO LONGER HAVE A HOME.
I WAS ONCE AMONG YOU, BUT NO MORE.
BUT
I MISS
YOU.

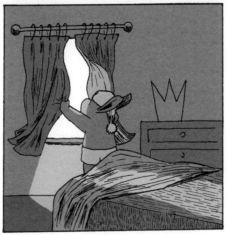

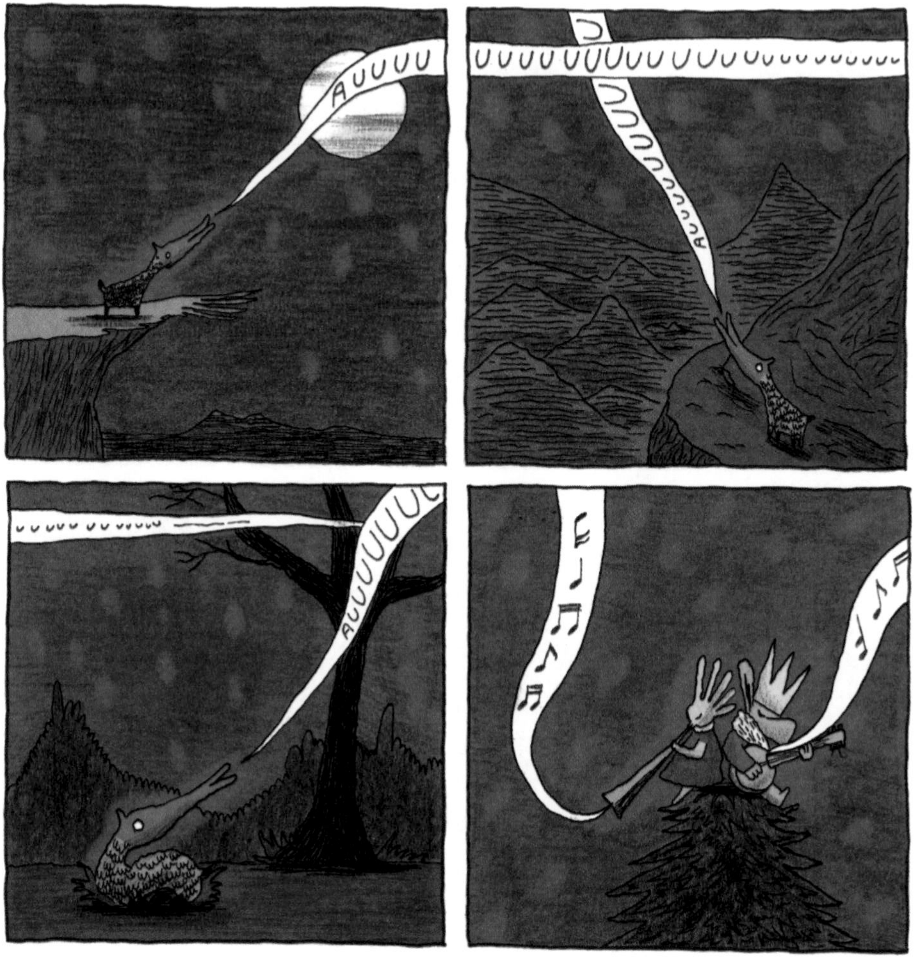
AUUUU

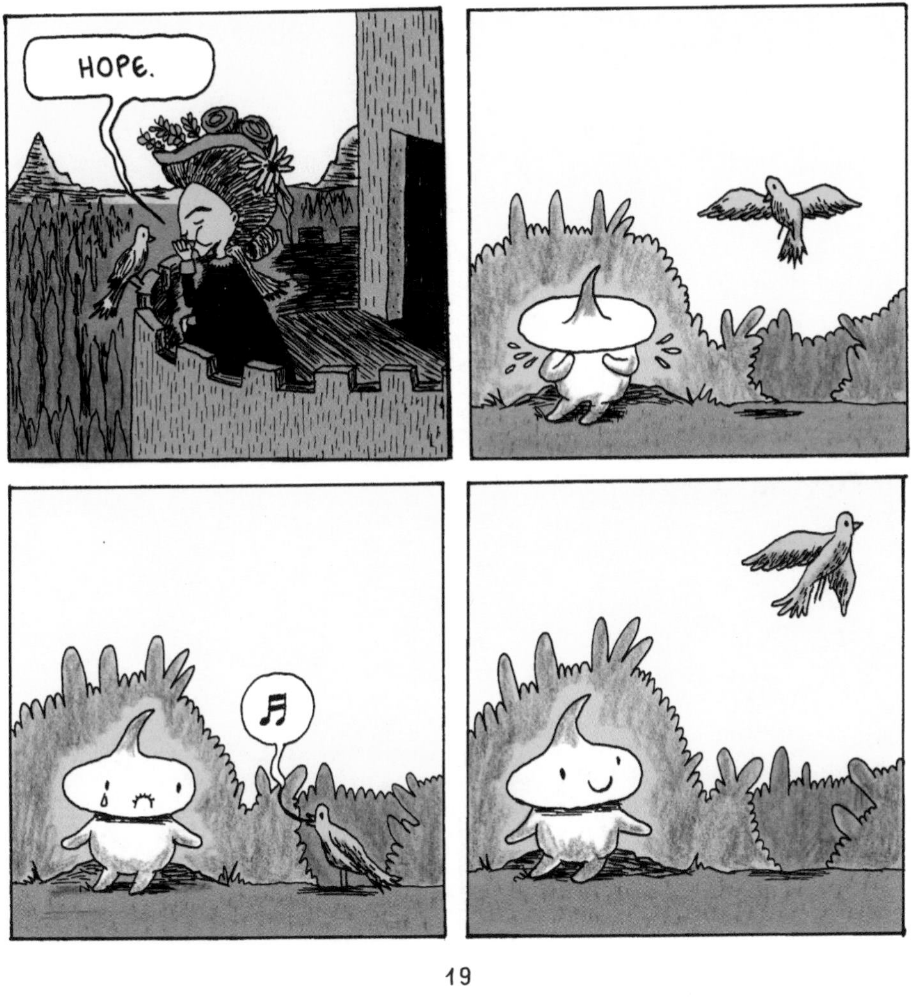
HOPE.
♬

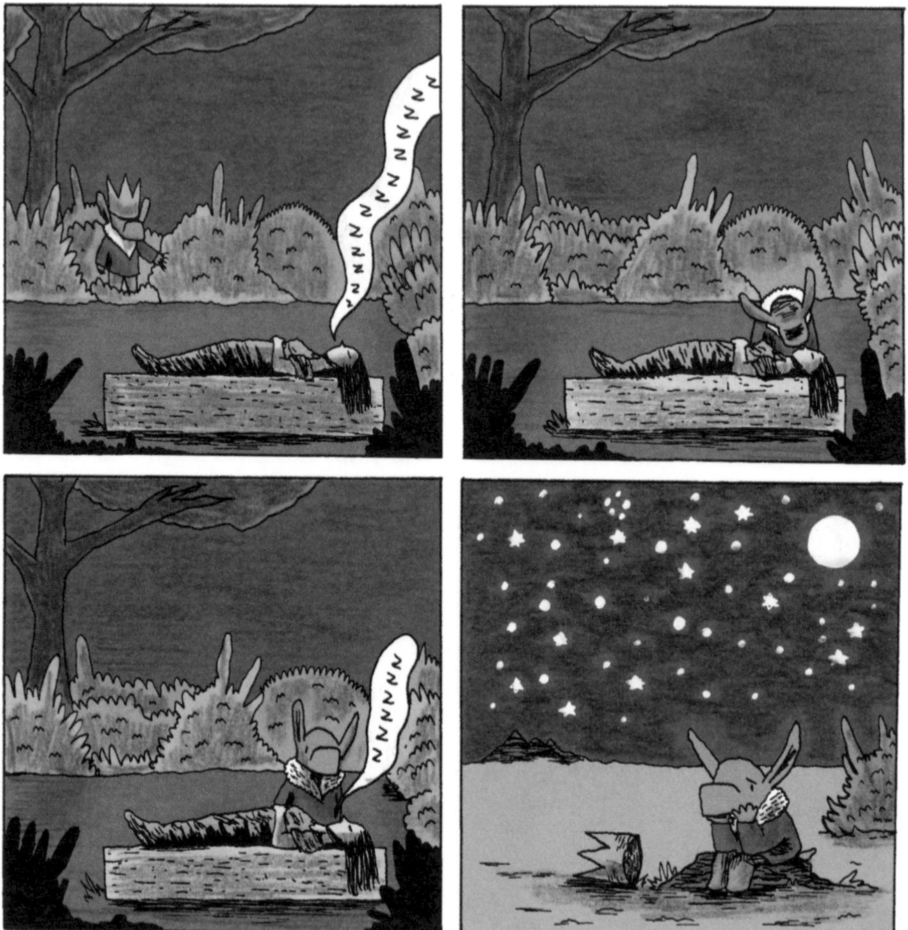
ZZZZZZZZZZZZZ
ZZZZZZ

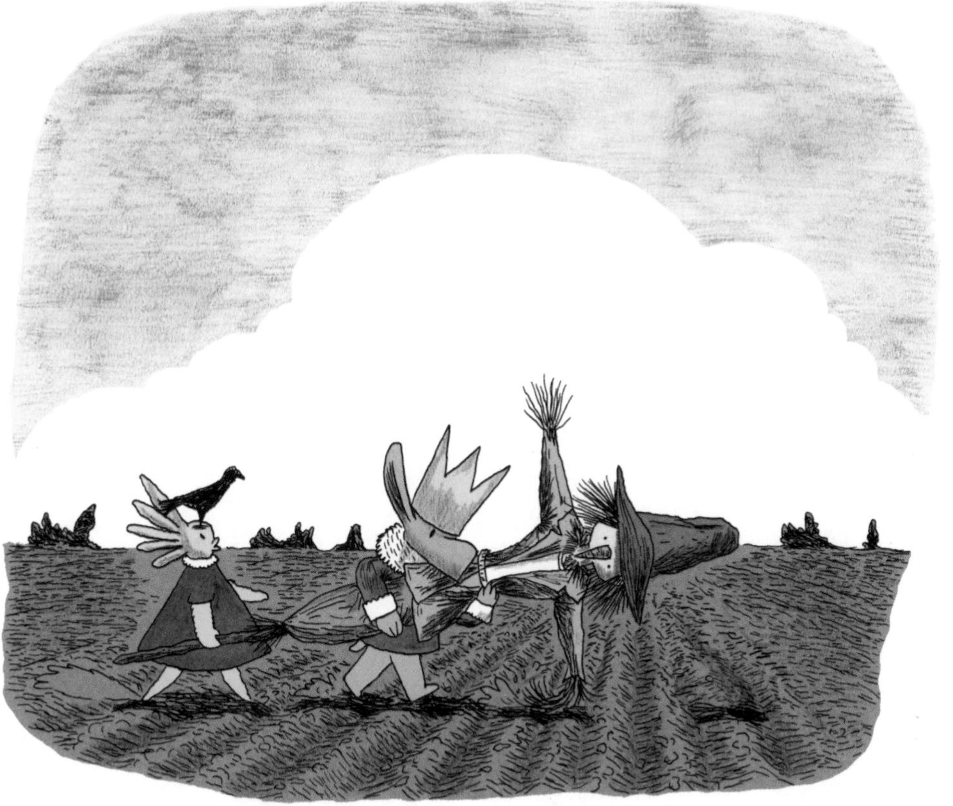

"I HAVE A FEELING THIS ISN'T GOING TO WORK!"

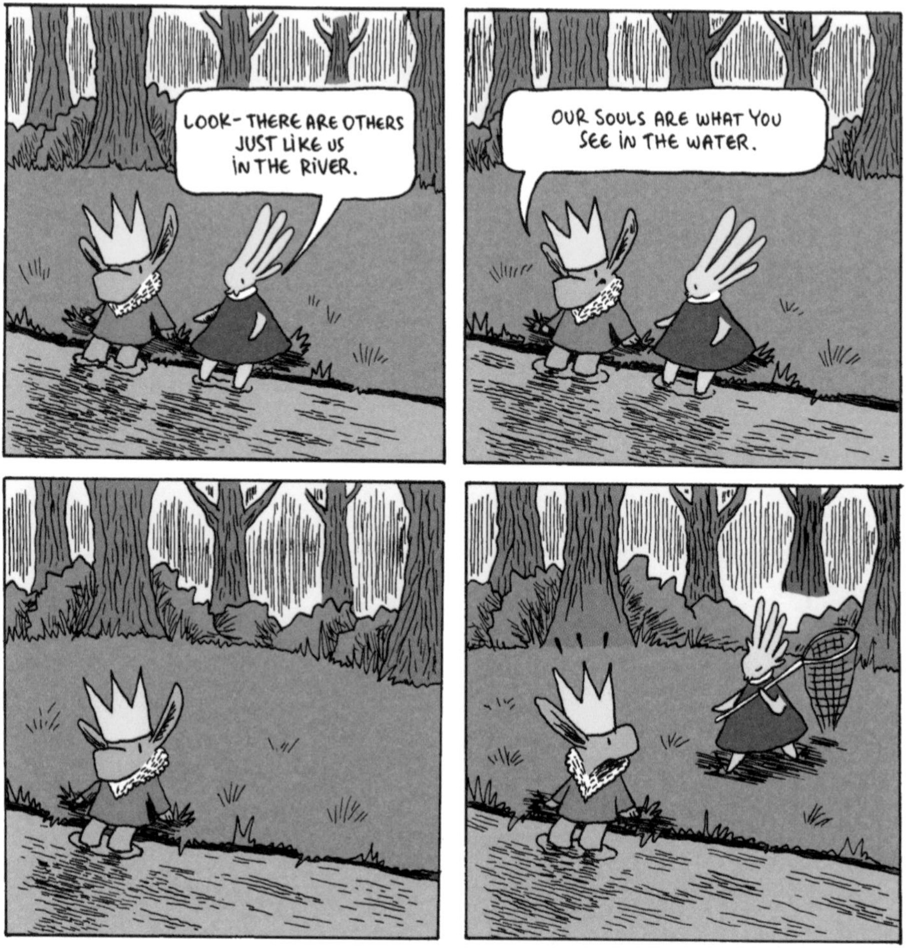
LOOK- THERE ARE OTHERS JUST LIKE US IN THE RIVER.
OUR SOULS ARE WHAT YOU SEE IN THE WATER.

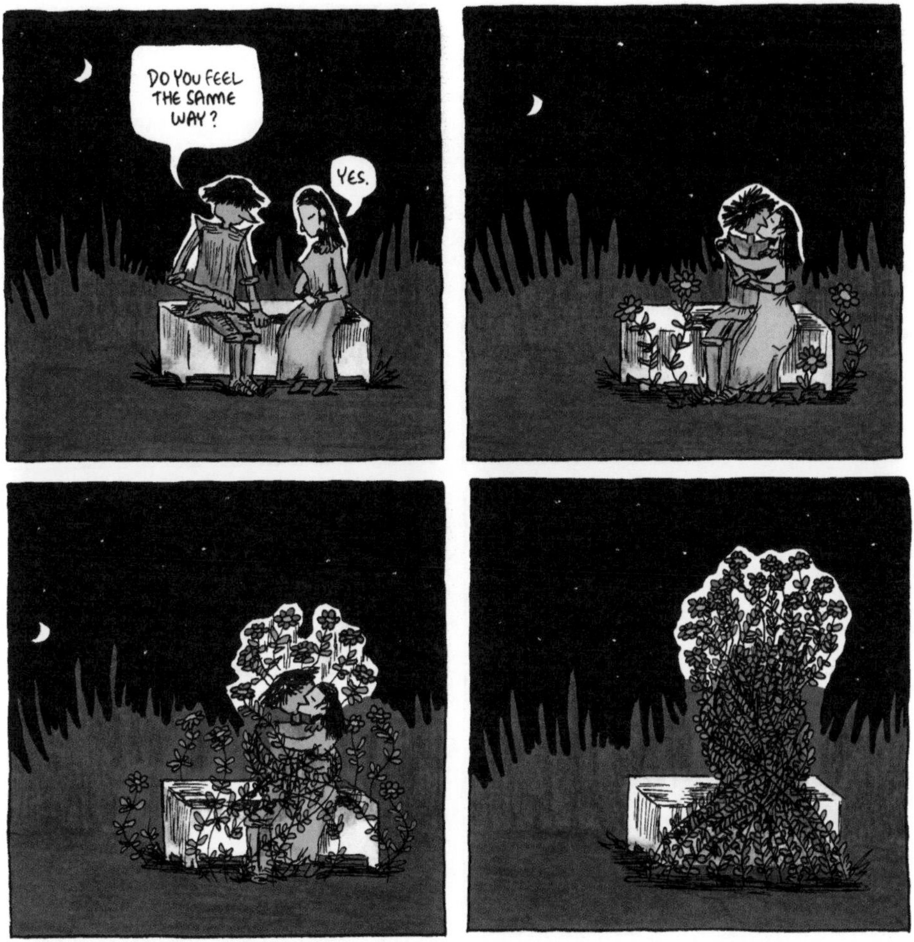
DO YOU FEEL THE SAME WAY?
YES.

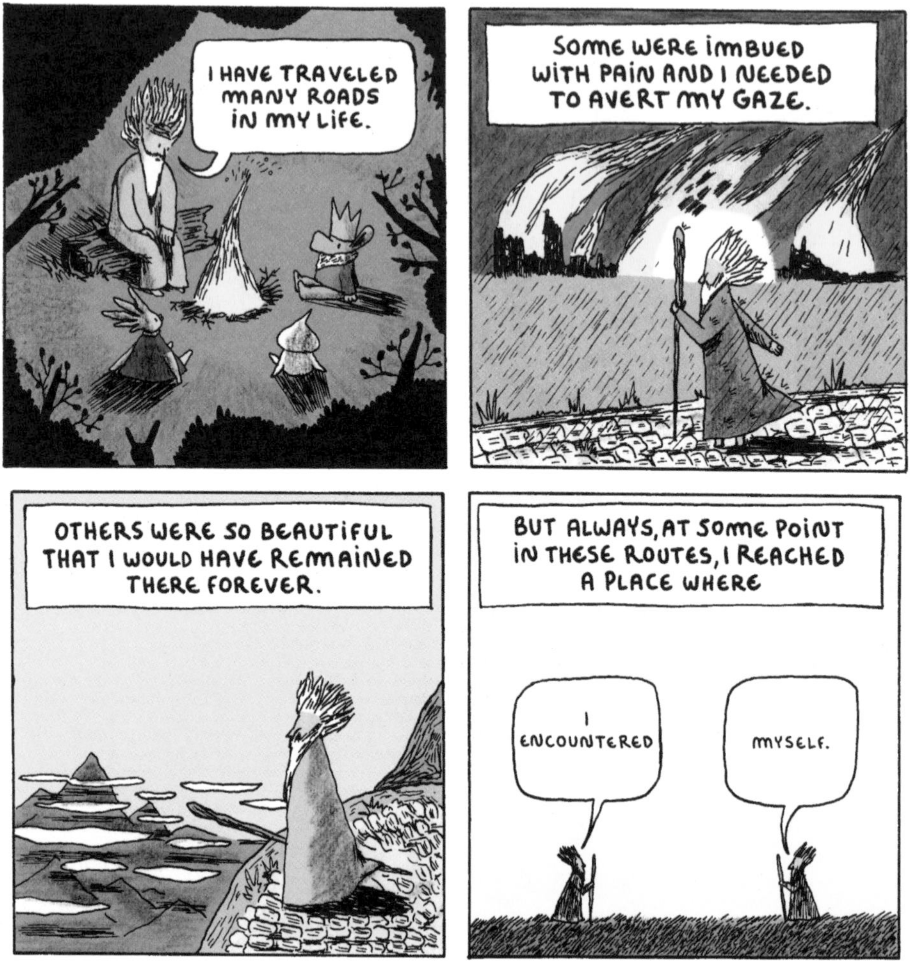
I HAVE TRAVELED MANY ROADS IN MY LIFE.
SOME WERE IMBUED WITH PAIN AND I NEEDED TO AVERT MY GAZE.
OTHERS WERE SO BEAUTIFUL THAT I WOULD HAVE REMAINED THERE FOREVER.
BUT ALWAYS, AT SOME POINT IN THESE ROUTES, I REACHED A PLACE WHERE
I ENCOUNTERED
MYSELF.

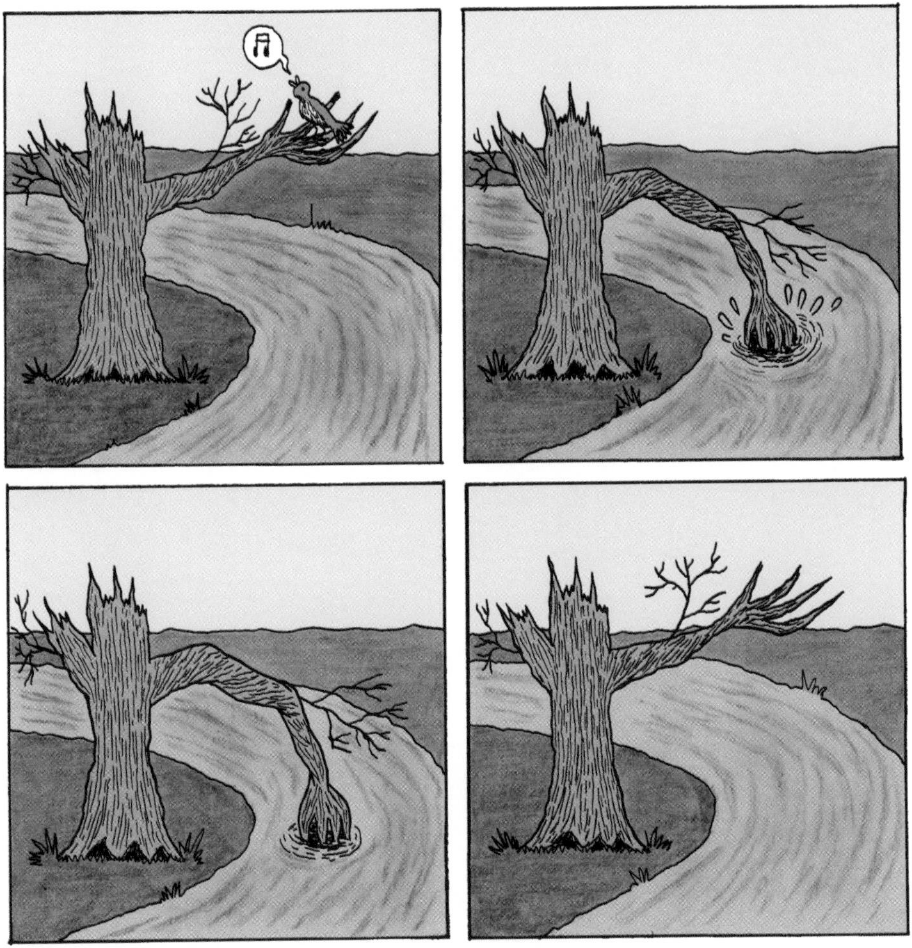

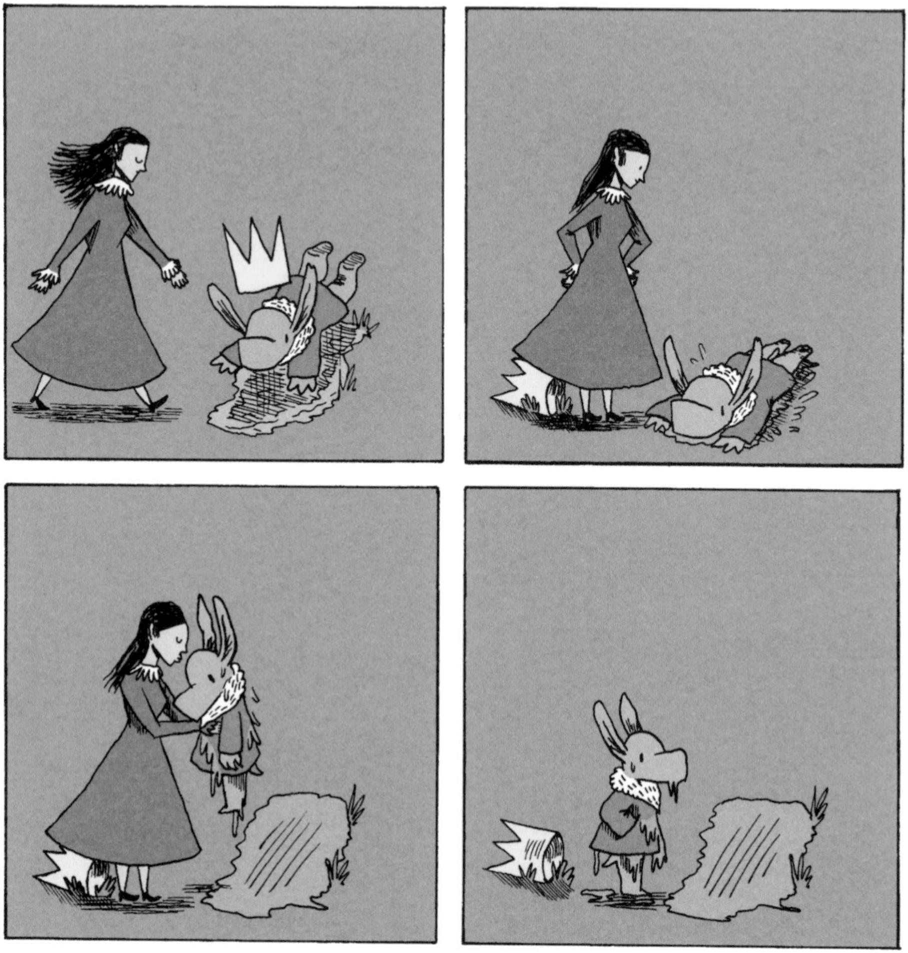

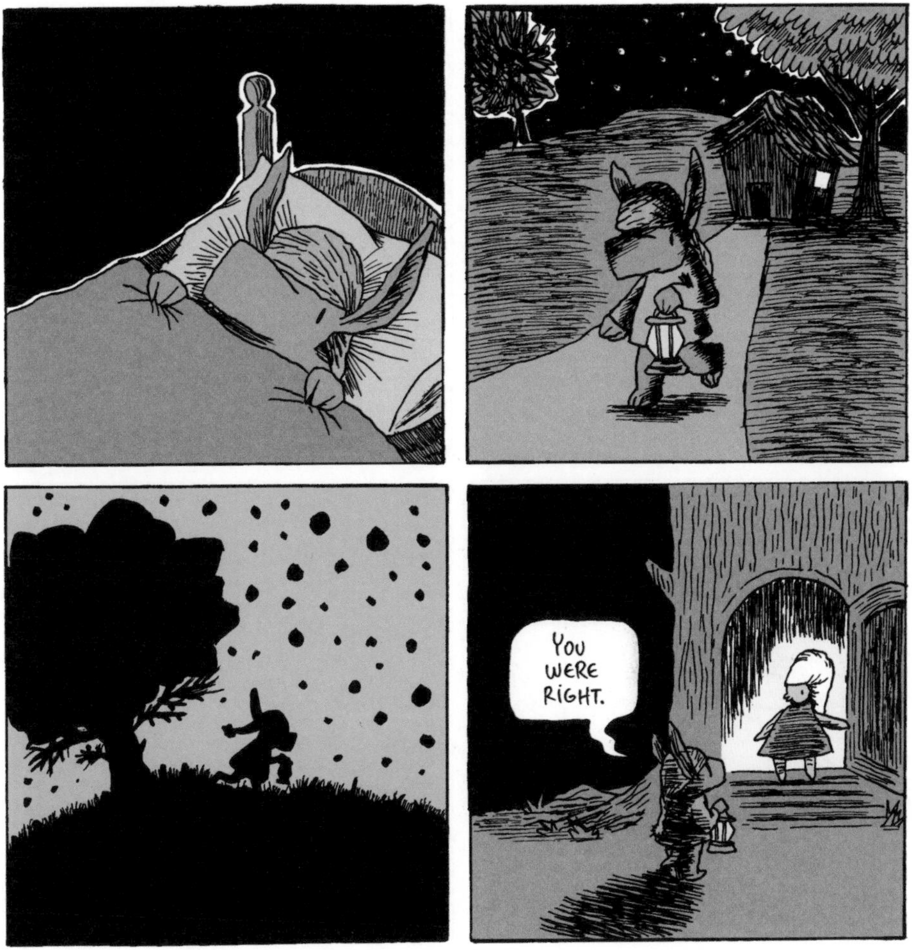
YOU WERE RIGHT.

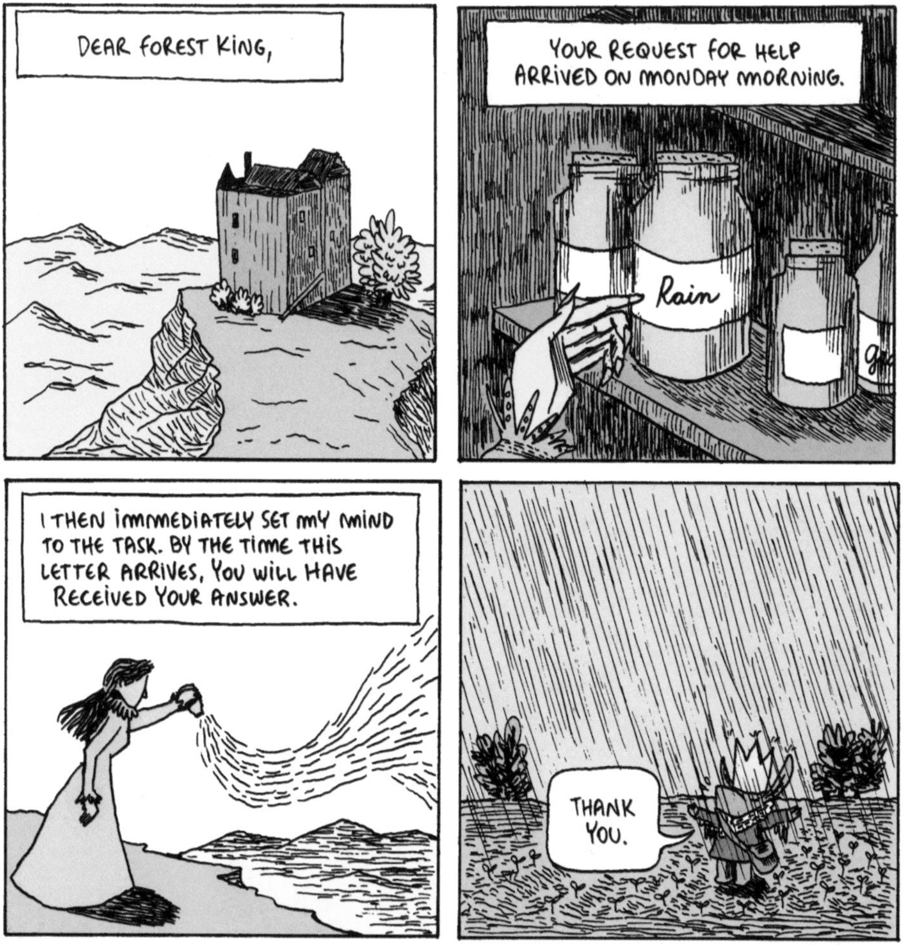
DEAR FOREST KING,
YOUR REQUEST FOR HELP ARRIVED ON MONDAY MORNING.
Rain
I THEN IMMEDIATELY SET MY MIND TO THE TASK. BY THE TIME THIS LETTER ARRIVES, YOU WILL HAVE RECEIVED YOUR ANSWER.
THANK YOU.

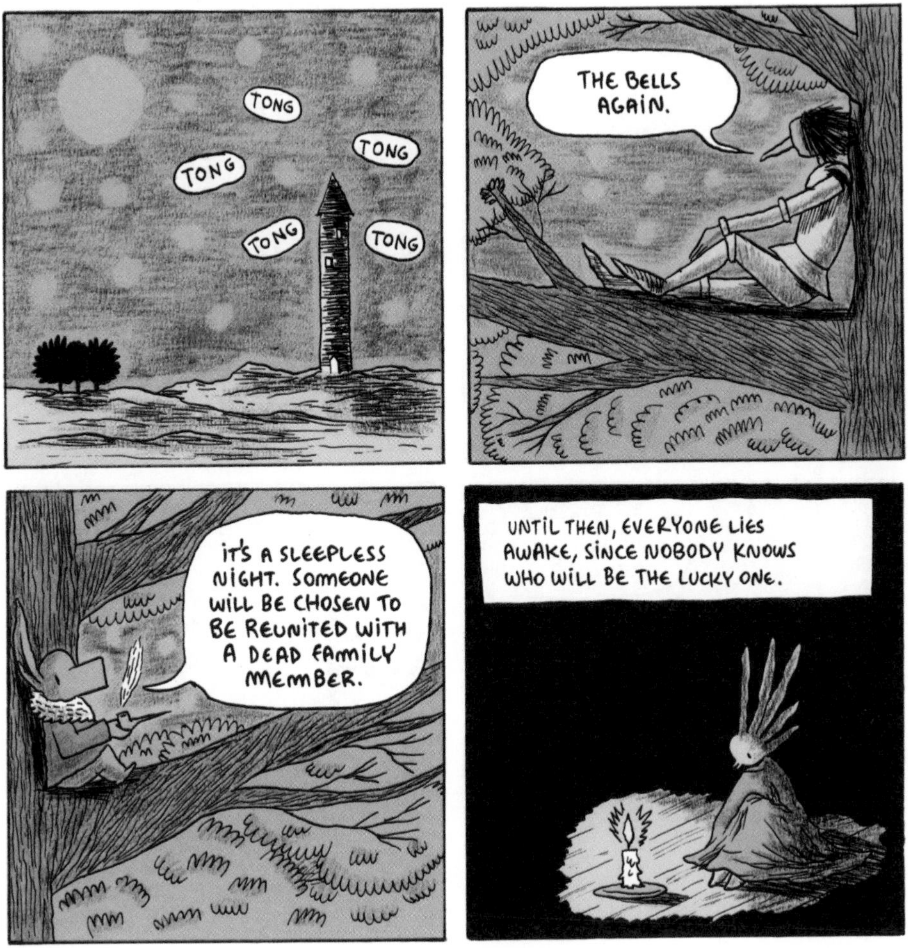
TONG
TONG
TONG
TONG
TONG
THE BELLS AGAIN.
IT'S A SLEEPLESS NIGHT. SOMEONE WILL BE CHOSEN TO BE REUNITED WITH A DEAD FAMILY MEMBER.
UNTIL THEN, EVERYONE LIES AWAKE, SINCE NOBODY KNOWS WHO WILL BE THE LUCKY ONE.

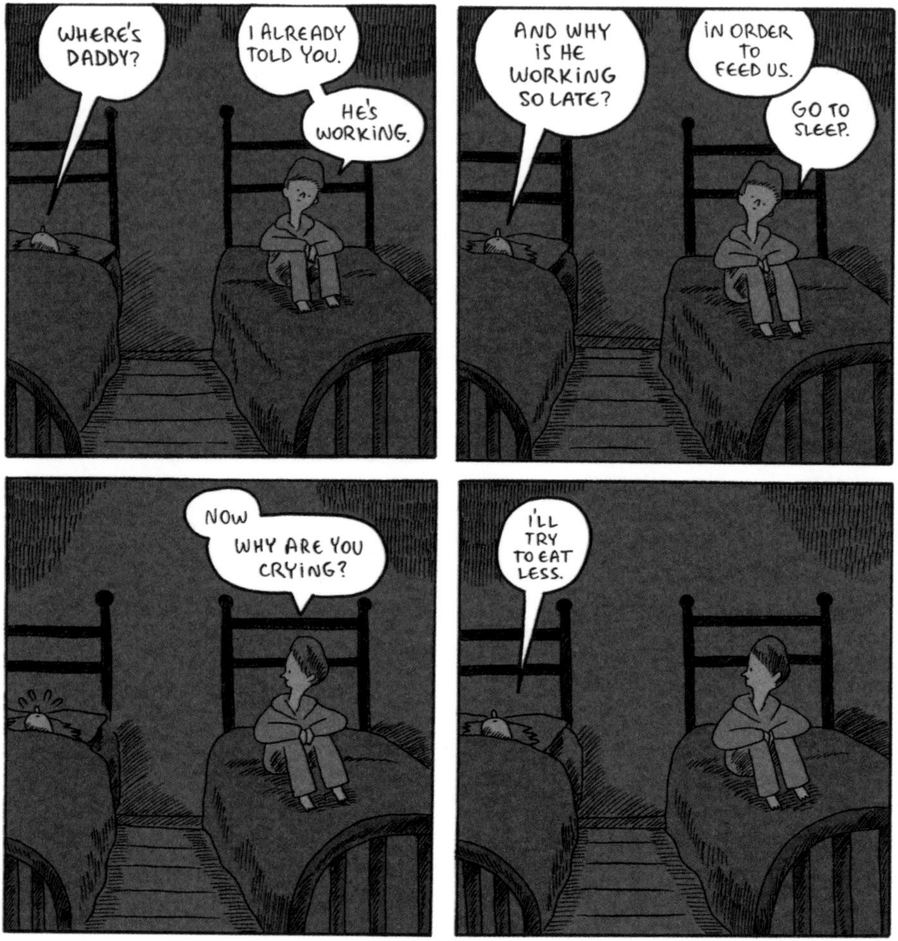
WHERE'S DADDY?
I ALREADY TOLD YOU.
HE'S WORKING.
AND WHY IS HE WORKING SO LATE?
IN ORDER TO FEED US.
GO TO SLEEP.
NOW
WHY ARE YOU CRYING?
I'LL TRY TO EAT LESS.

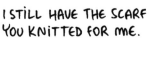
"THESE DAYS HAVE BEEN PARTICULARLY COLD.

I STILL HAVE THE SCARF YOU KNITTED FOR ME.

YOUR SCENT HAS BECOME ATTACHED TO IT.

AND WHEN I WEAR IT, I FEEL THAT YOU ARE STILL WITH ME."

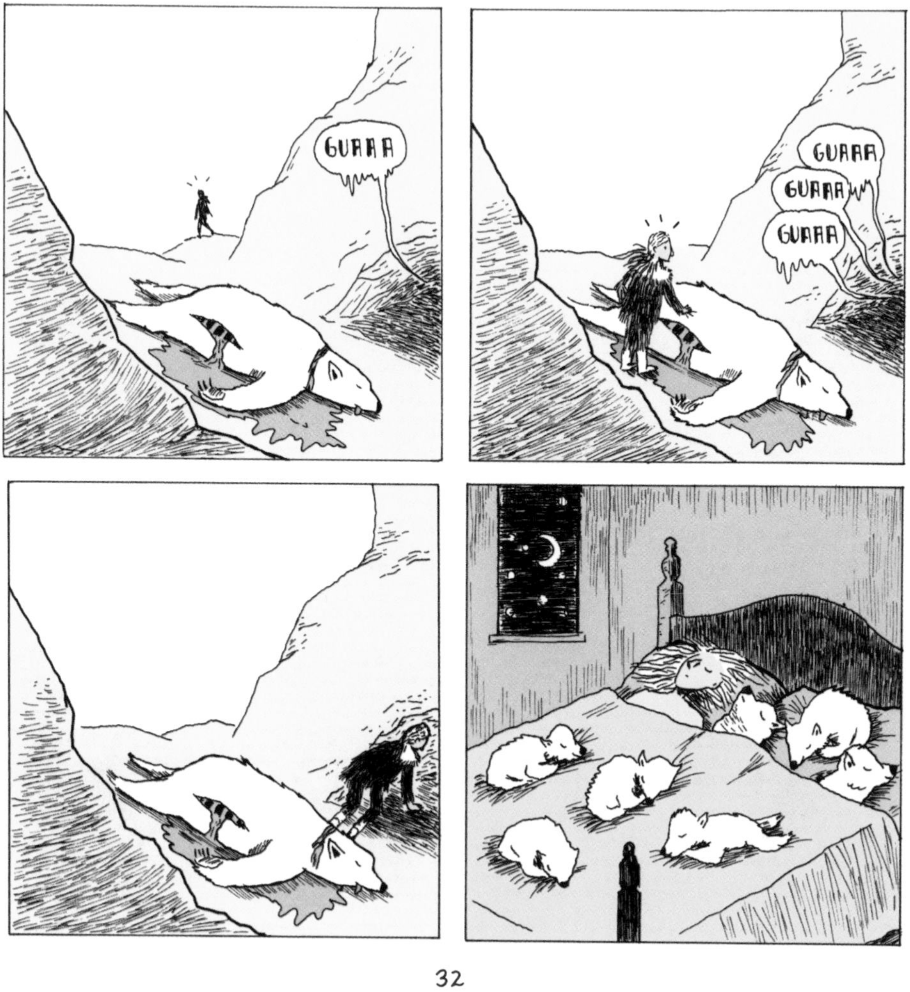
GURRR
GURRR
GURRR
GURRR

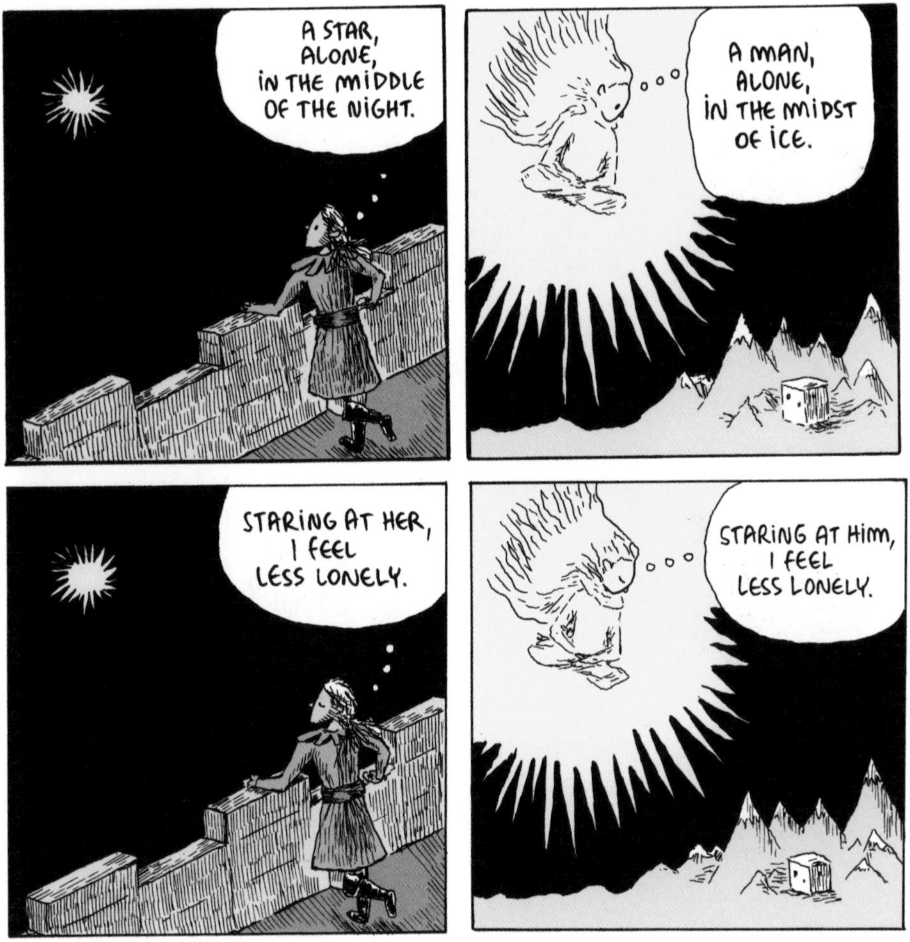
A STAR,
ALONE,
IN THE MIDDLE
OF THE NIGHT.
A MAN,
ALONE,
IN THE MIDST
OF ICE.
STARING AT HER,
I FEEL
LESS LONELY.
STARING AT HIM,
I FEEL
LESS LONELY.

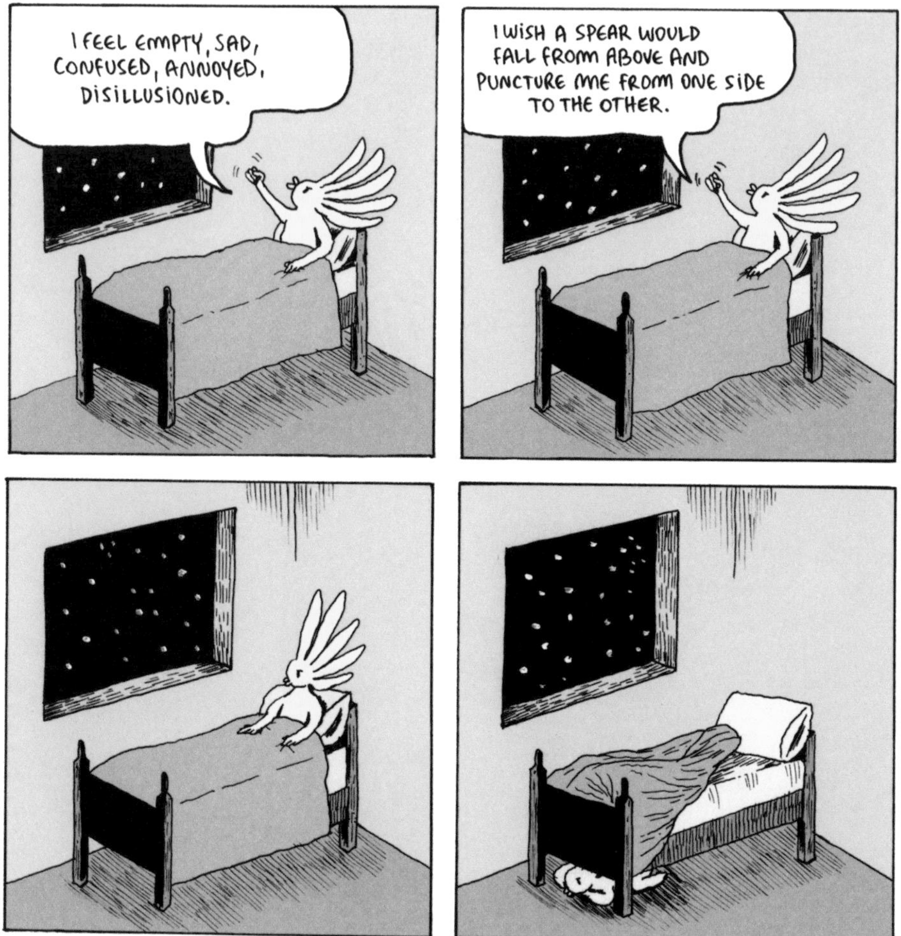
I FEEL EMPTY, SAD, CONFUSED, ANNOYED, DISILLUSIONED.
I WISH A SPEAR WOULD FALL FROM ABOVE AND PUNCTURE ME FROM ONE SIDE TO THE OTHER.

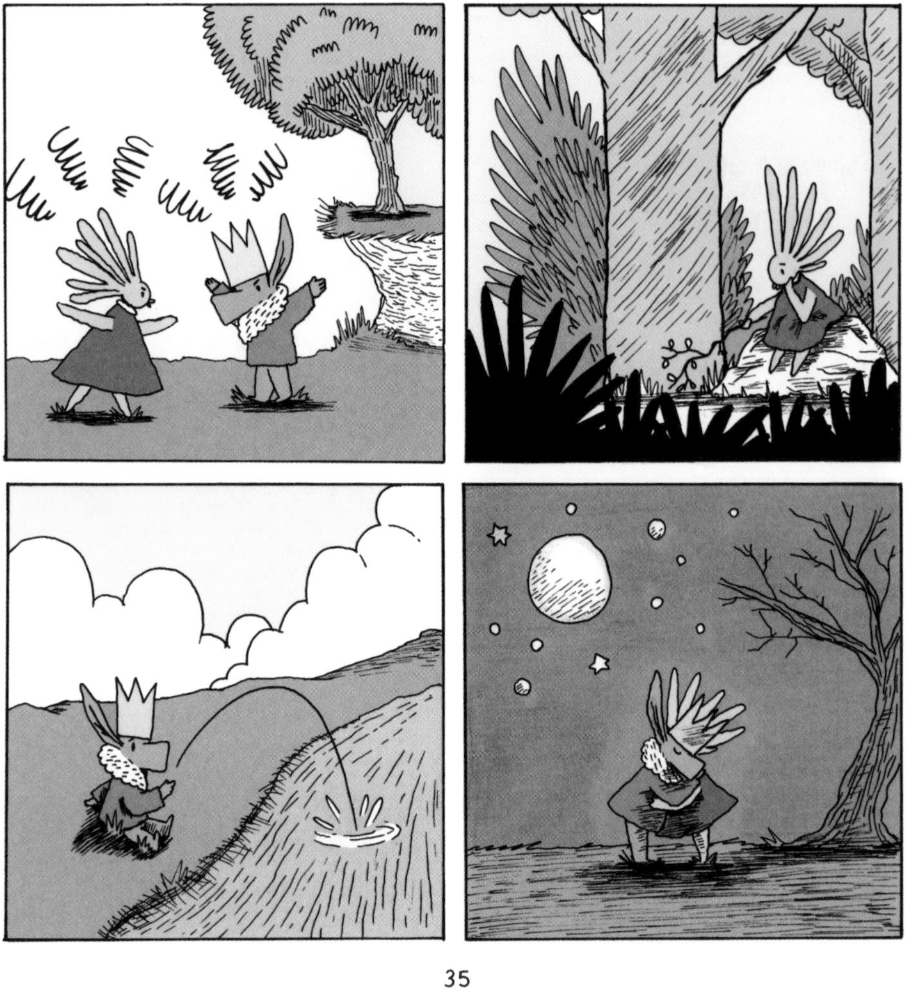

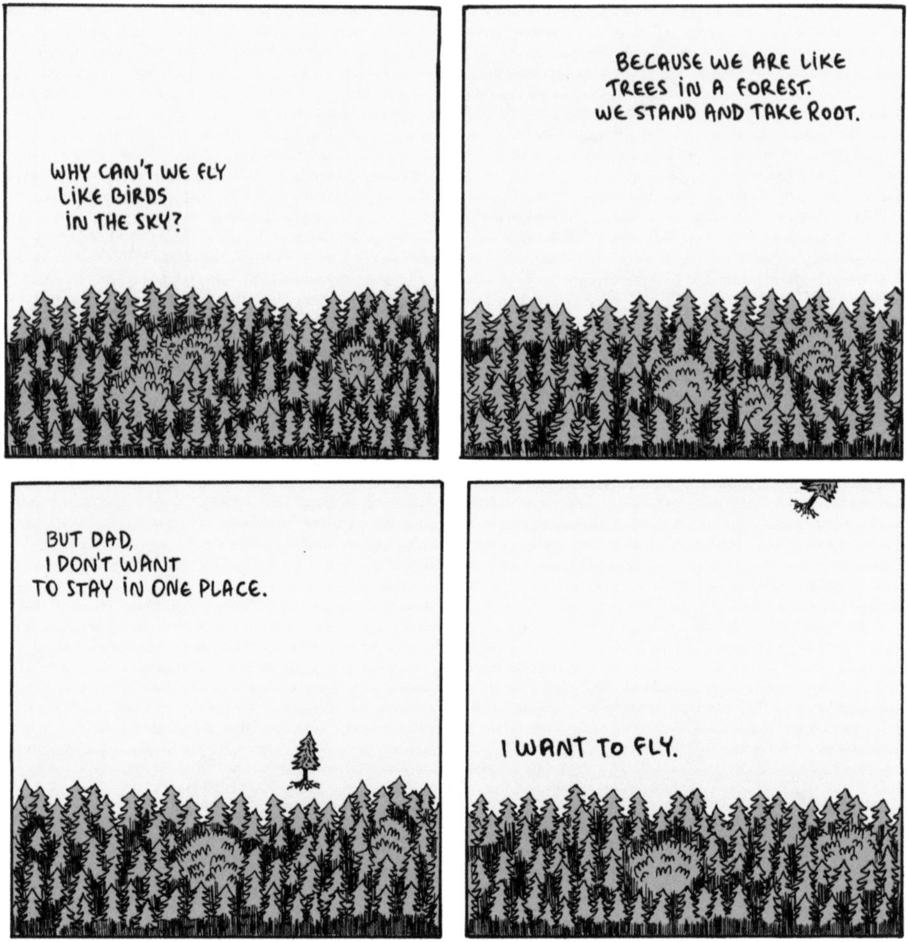
WHY CAN'T WE FLY
LIKE BIRDS
IN THE SKY?
BECAUSE WE ARE LIKE
TREES IN A FOREST.
WE STAND AND TAKE ROOT.
BUT DAD,
I DON'T WANT
TO STAY IN ONE PLACE.
I WANT TO FLY.

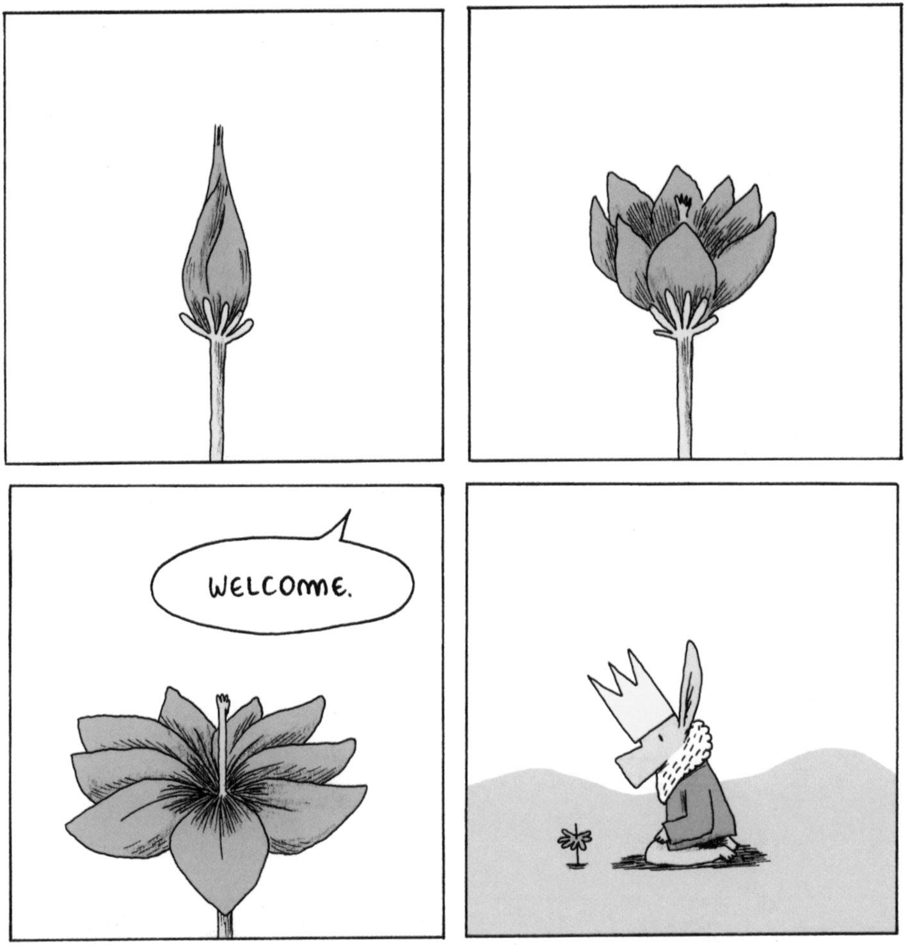
WELCOME.

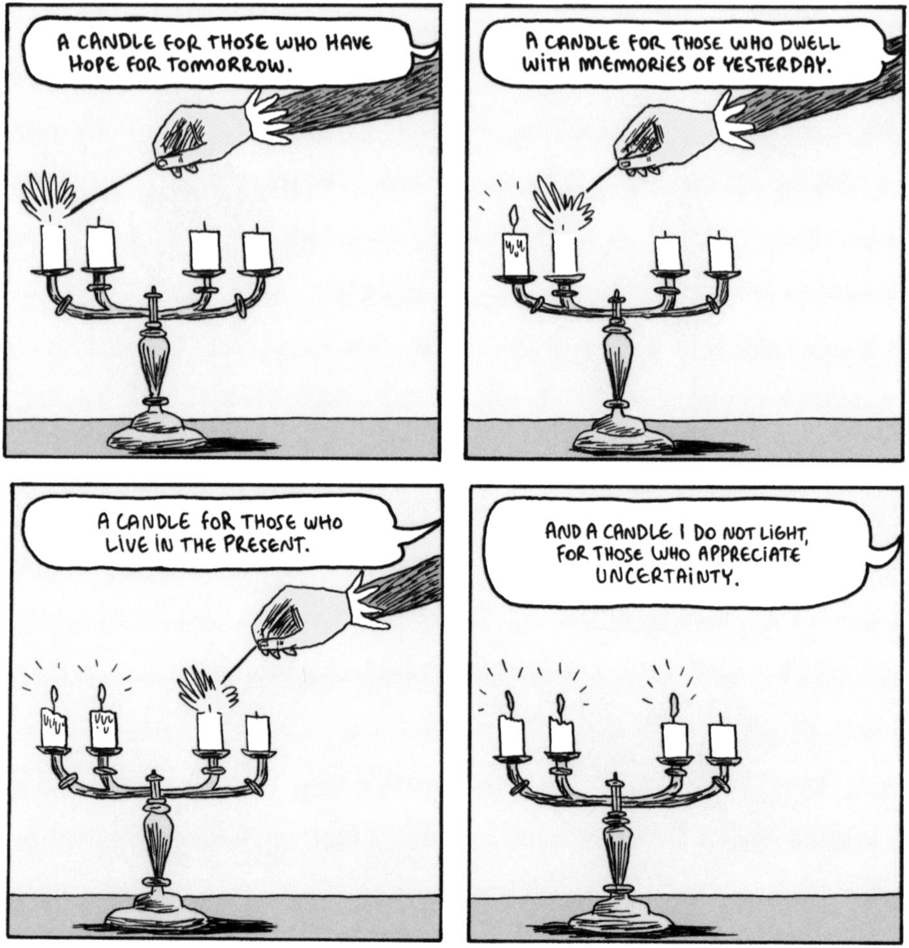
A CANDLE FOR THOSE WHO HAVE HOPE FOR TOMORROW.
A CANDLE FOR THOSE WHO DWELL WITH MEMORIES OF YESTERDAY.
A CANDLE FOR THOSE WHO LIVE IN THE PRESENT.
AND A CANDLE I DO NOT LIGHT, FOR THOSE WHO APPRECIATE UNCERTAINTY.

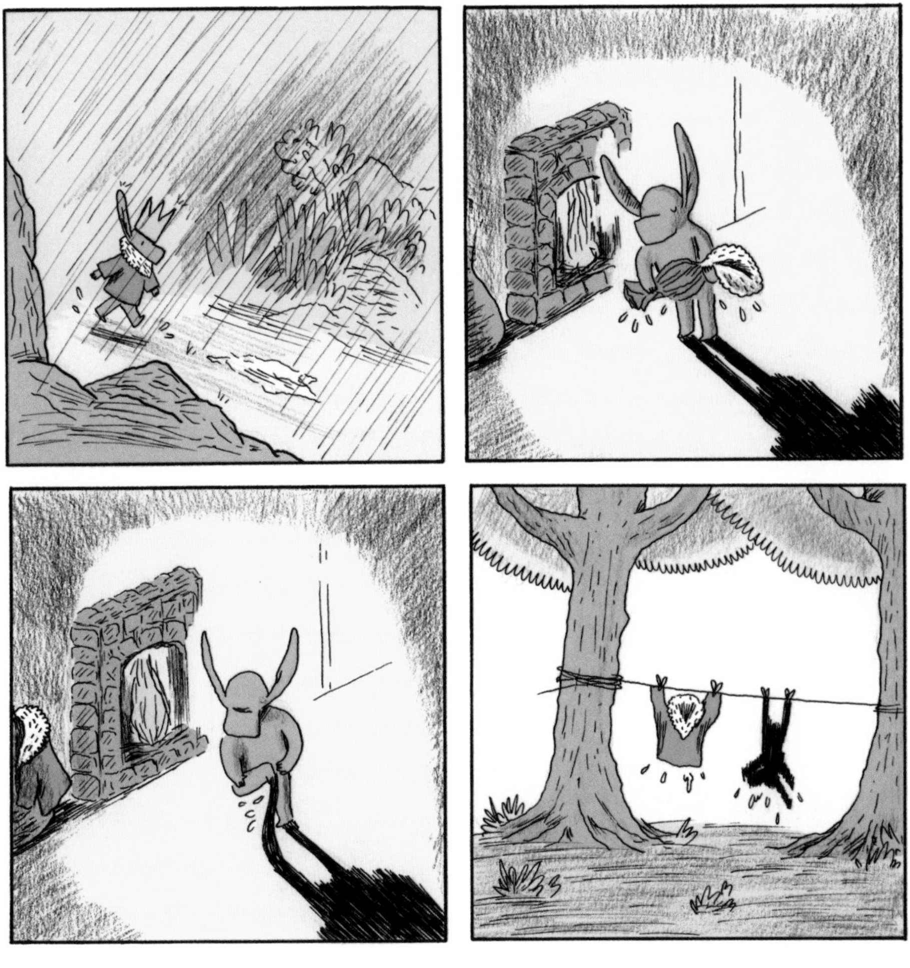

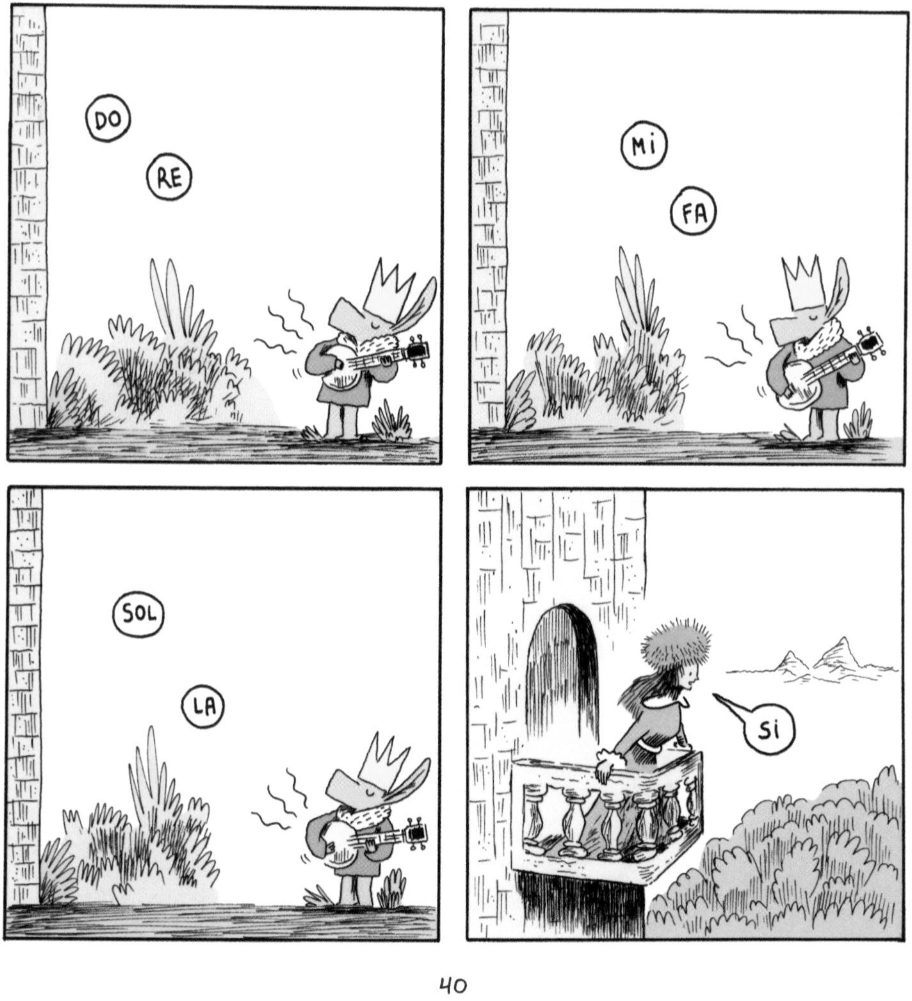
DO
RE
MI
FA
SOL
LA
SI

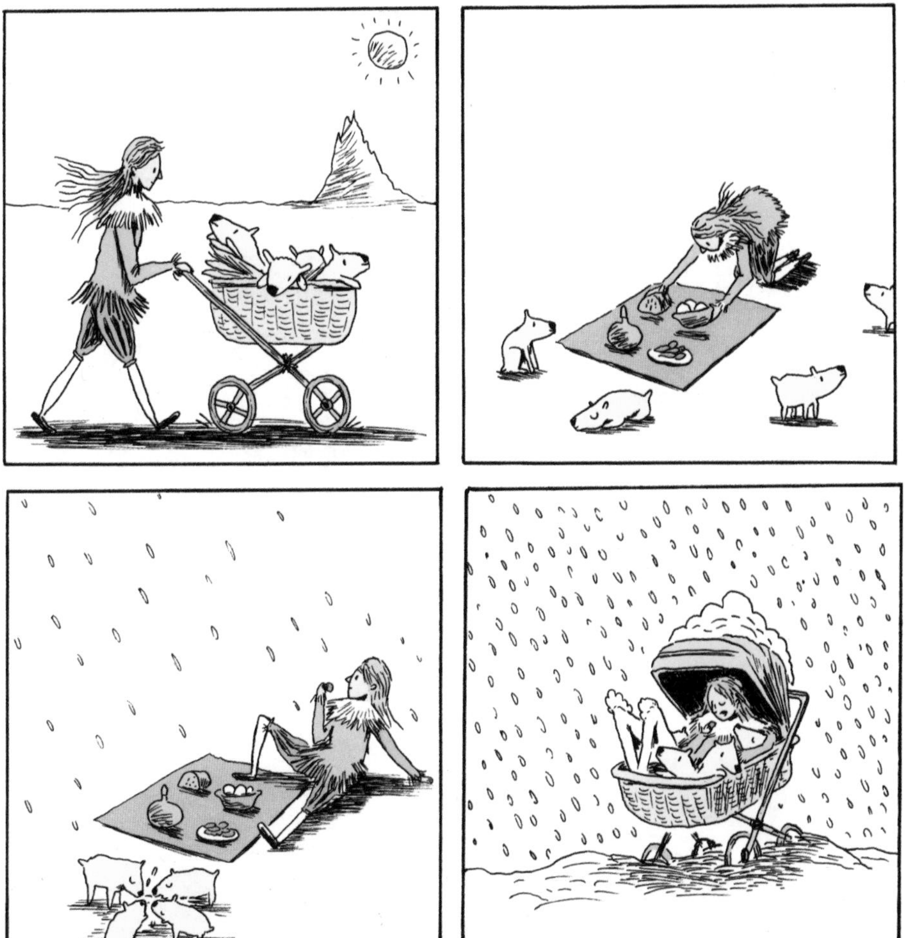

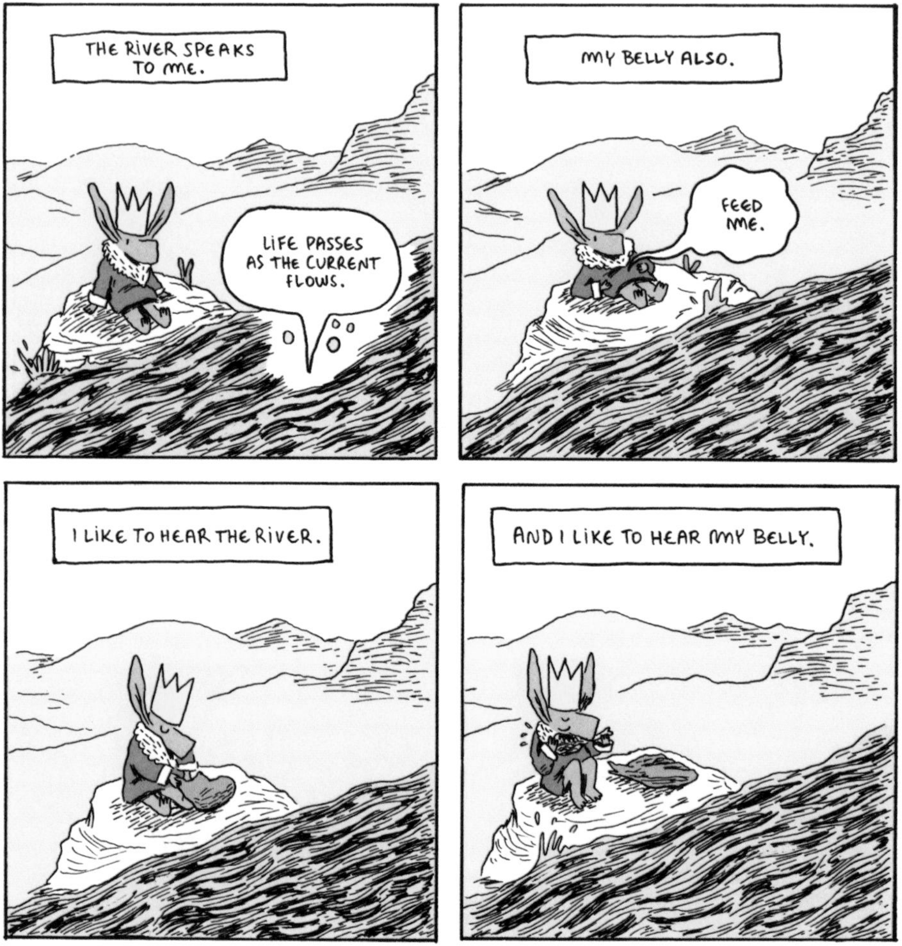
THE RIVER SPEAKS TO ME.
LIFE PASSES AS THE CURRENT FLOWS.
MY BELLY ALSO.
FEED ME.
I LIKE TO HEAR THE RIVER.
AND I LIKE TO HEAR MY BELLY.

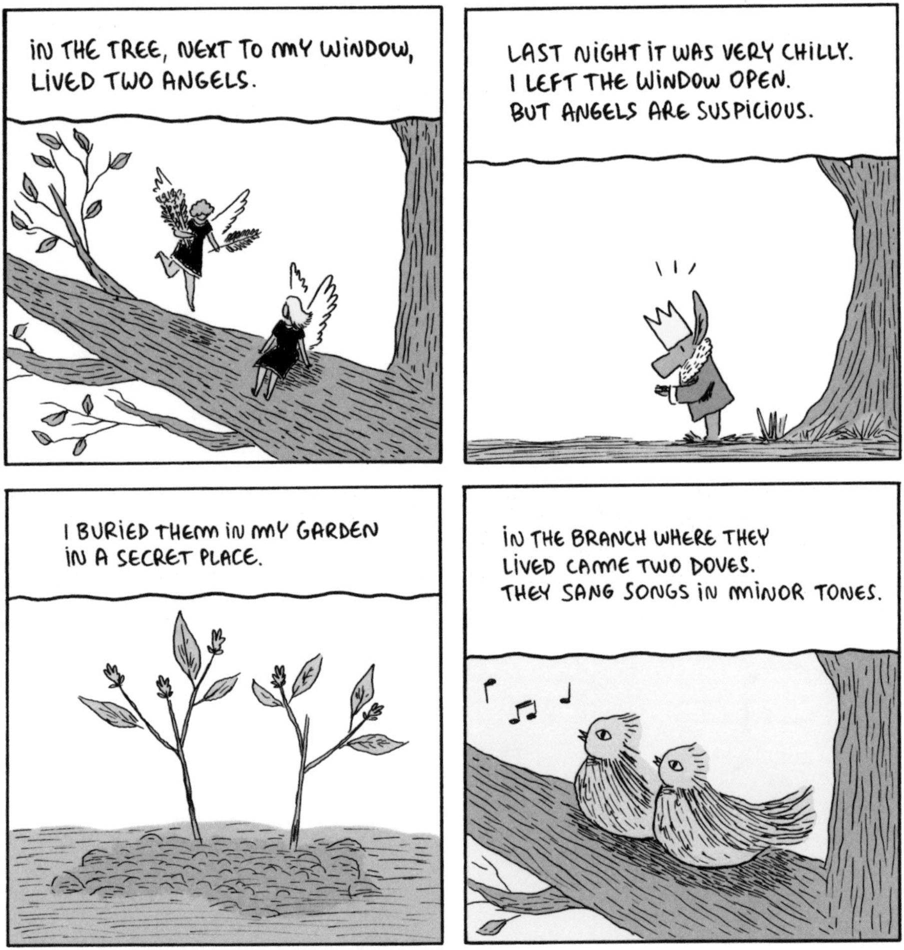
IN THE TREE, NEXT TO MY WINDOW, LIVED TWO ANGELS.
LAST NIGHT IT WAS VERY CHILLY. I LEFT THE WINDOW OPEN. BUT ANGELS ARE SUSPICIOUS.
I BURIED THEM IN MY GARDEN IN A SECRET PLACE.
IN THE BRANCH WHERE THEY LIVED CAME TWO DOVES. THEY SANG SONGS IN MINOR TONES.

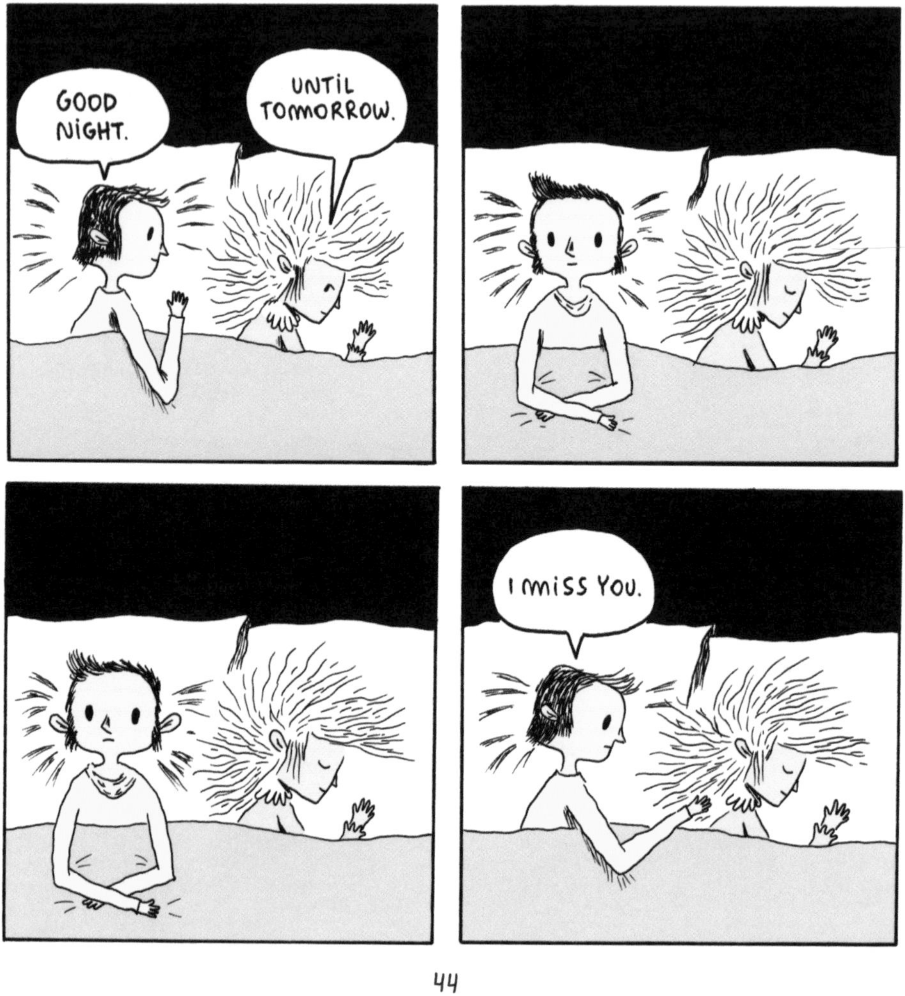
GOOD NIGHT.
UNTIL TOMORROW.
I MISS YOU.

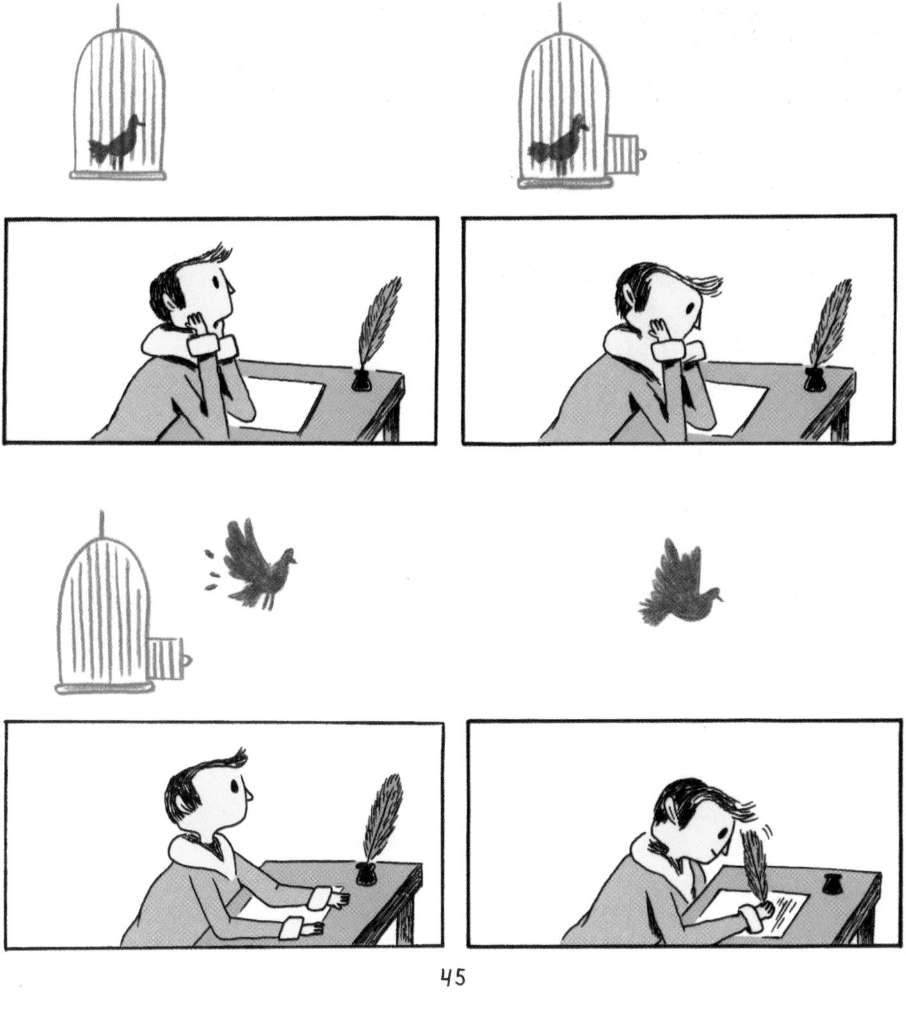

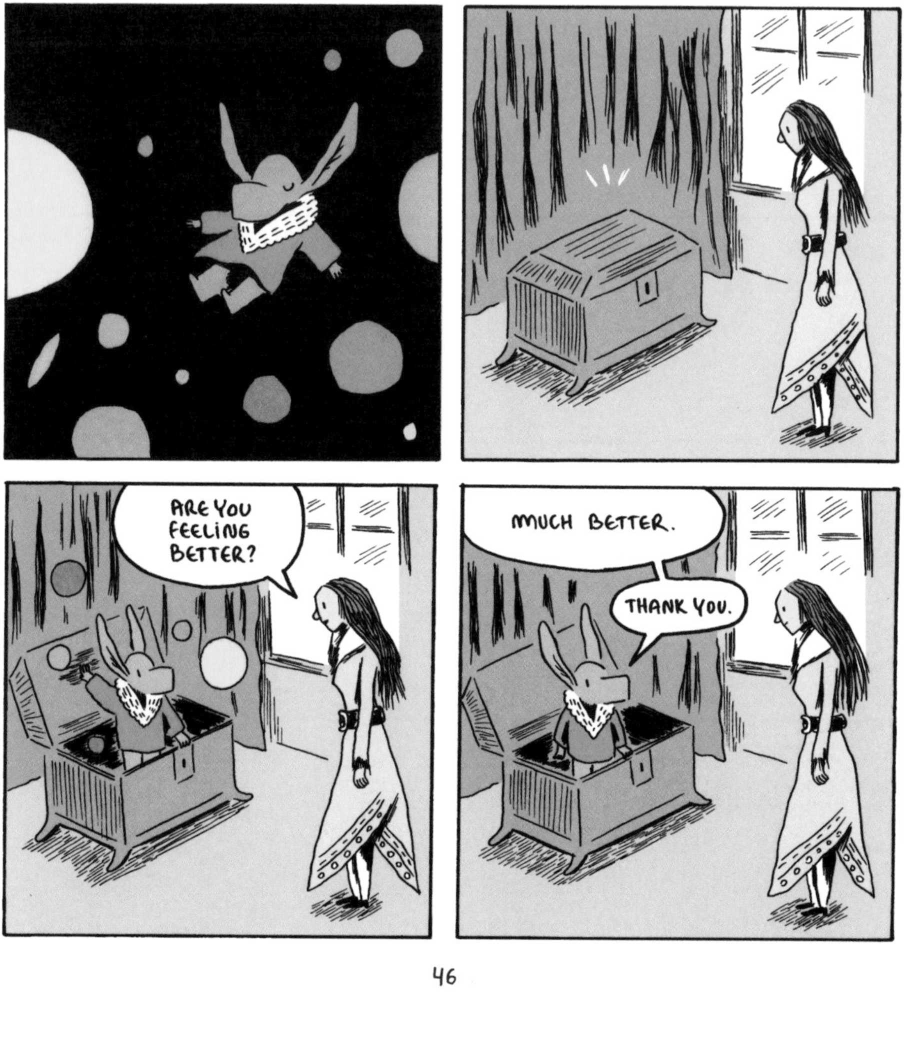
ARE YOU
FEELING
BETTER?
MUCH BETTER.
THANK YOU.

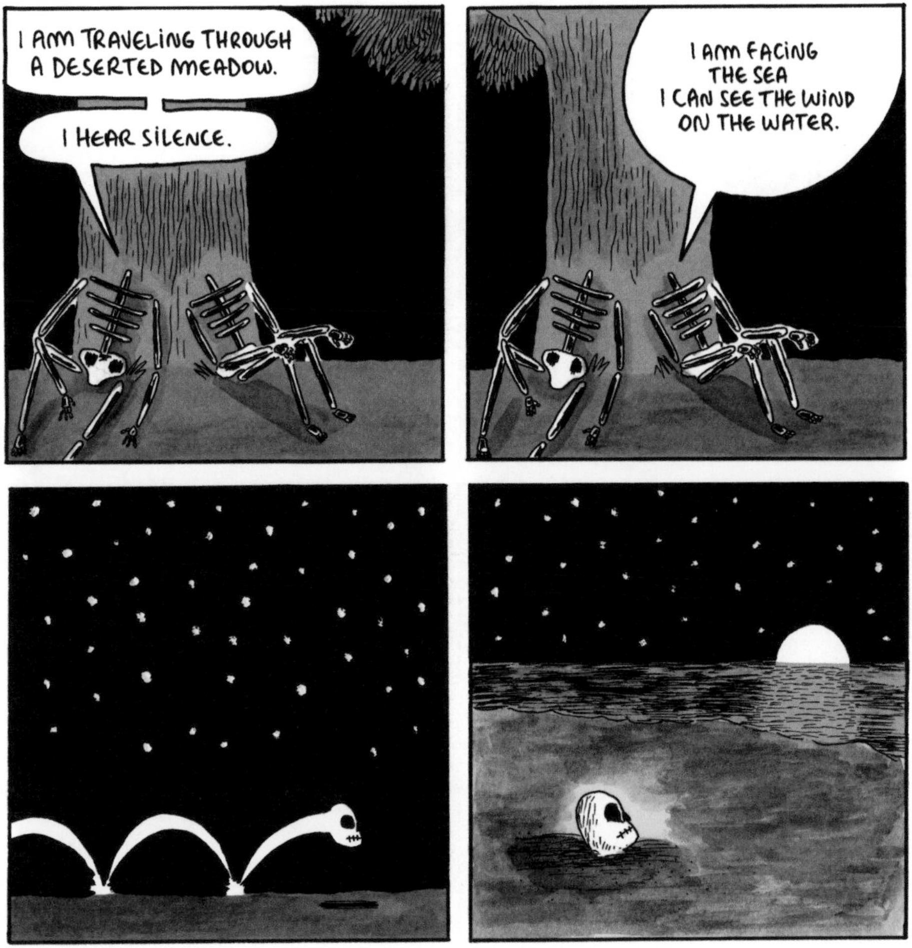
I AM TRAVELING THROUGH A DESERTED MEADOW.
I HEAR SILENCE.
I AM FACING THE SEA I CAN SEE THE WIND ON THE WATER.

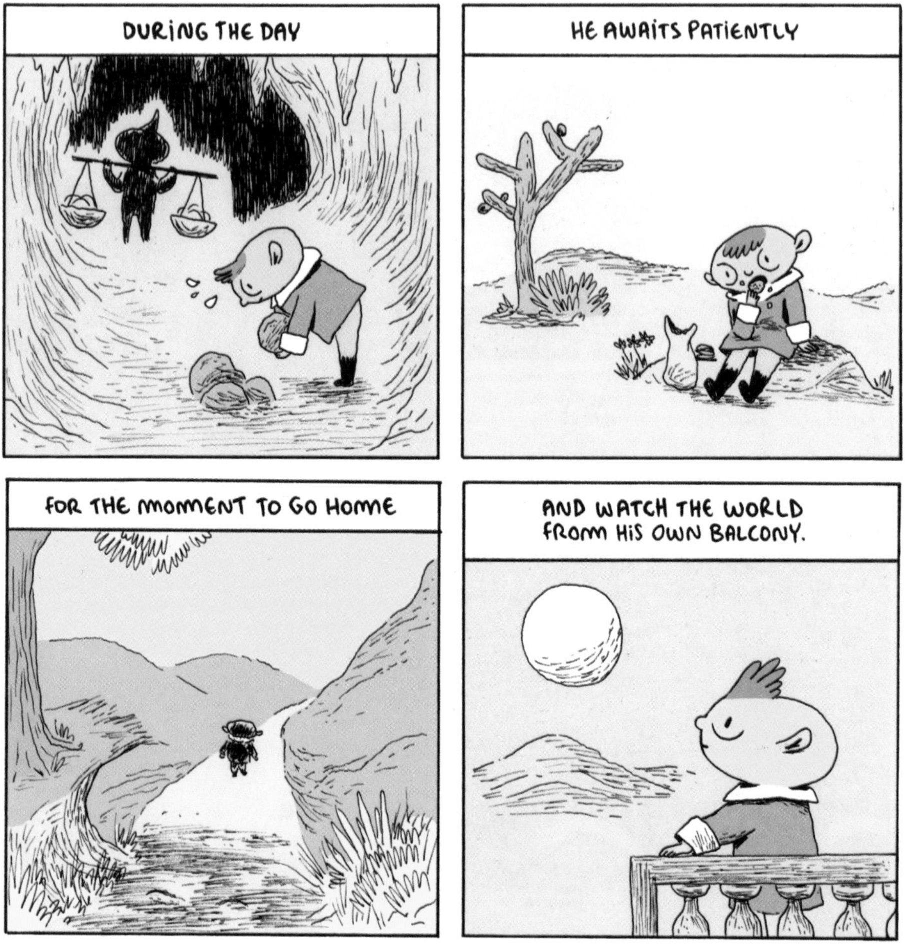
DURING THE DAY
HE AWAITS PATIENTLY
FOR THE MOMENT TO GO HOME
AND WATCH THE WORLD FROM HIS OWN BALCONY.

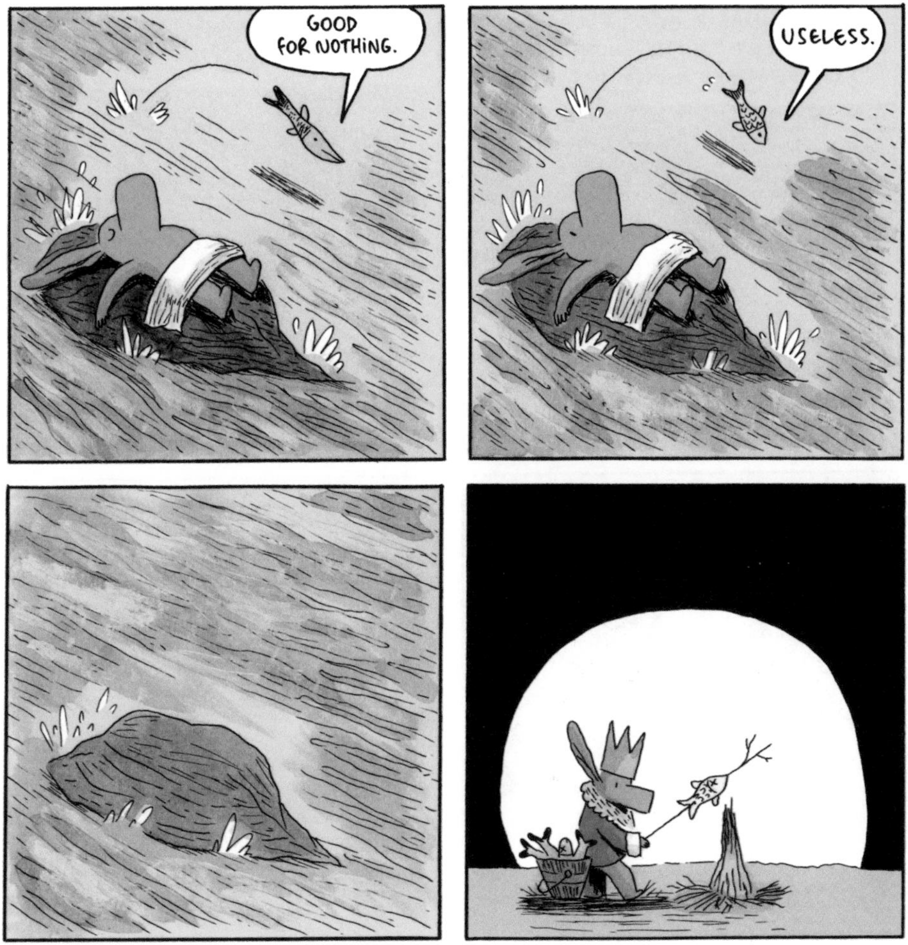
GOOD FOR NOTHING.
USELESS.

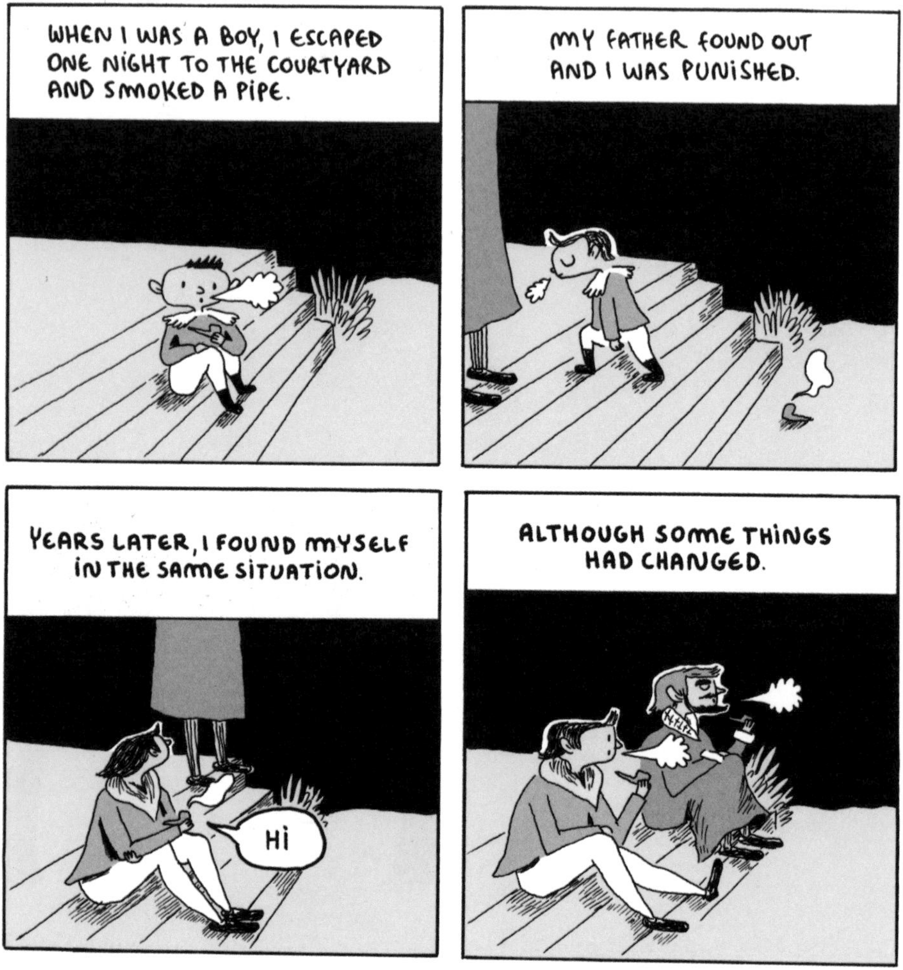
WHEN I WAS A BOY, I ESCAPED ONE NIGHT TO THE COURTYARD AND SMOKED A PIPE.
MY FATHER FOUND OUT AND I WAS PUNISHED.
YEARS LATER, I FOUND MYSELF IN THE SAME SITUATION.
Hi
ALTHOUGH SOME THINGS HAD CHANGED.

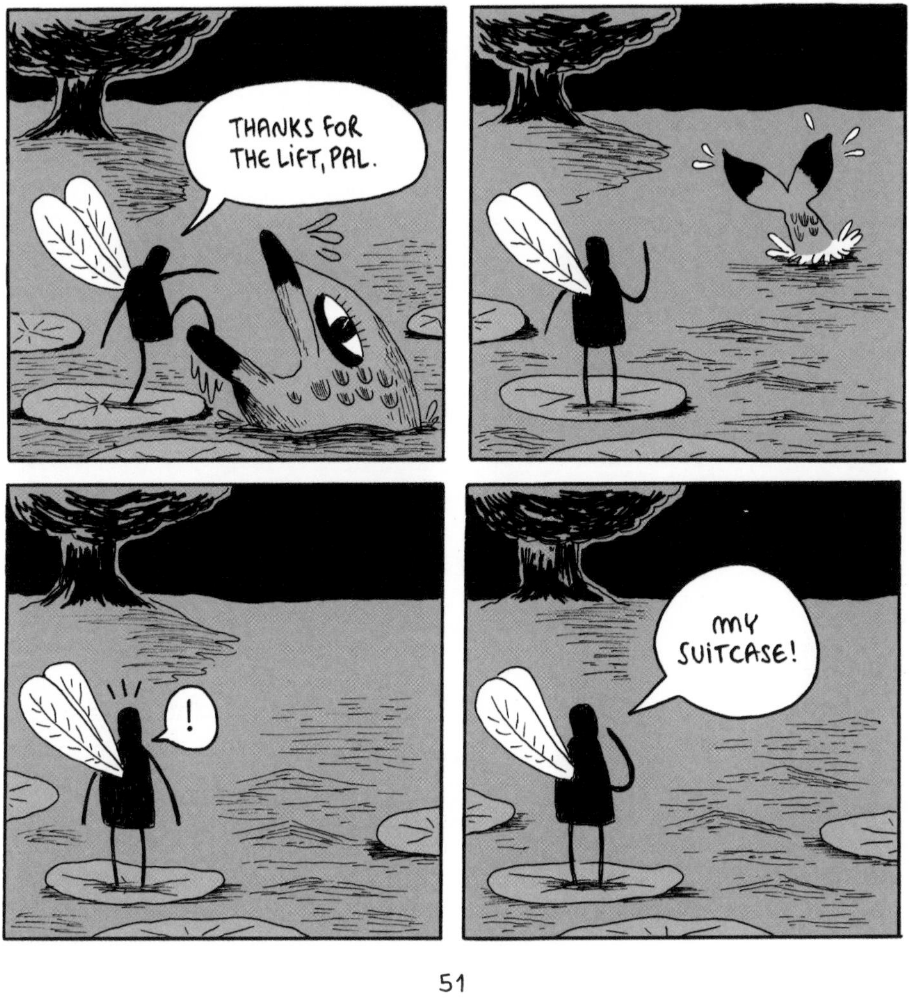
THANKS FOR THE LIFT, PAL.
!
MY SUITCASE!

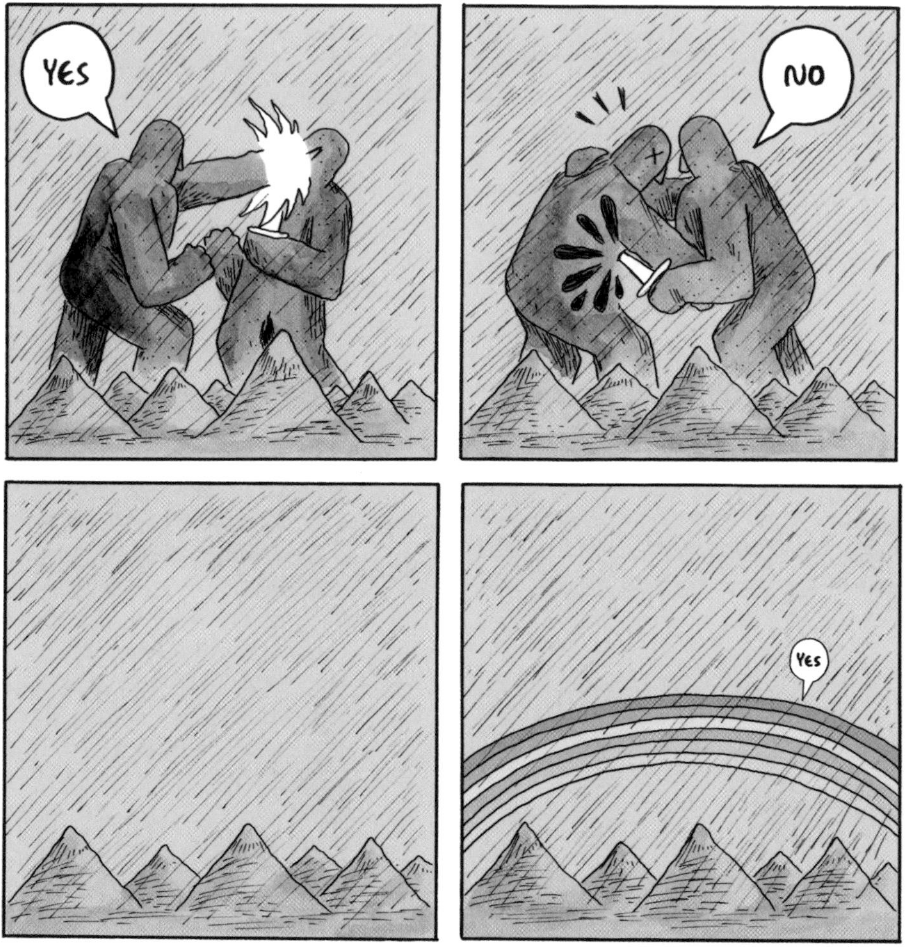
YES
NO
YES

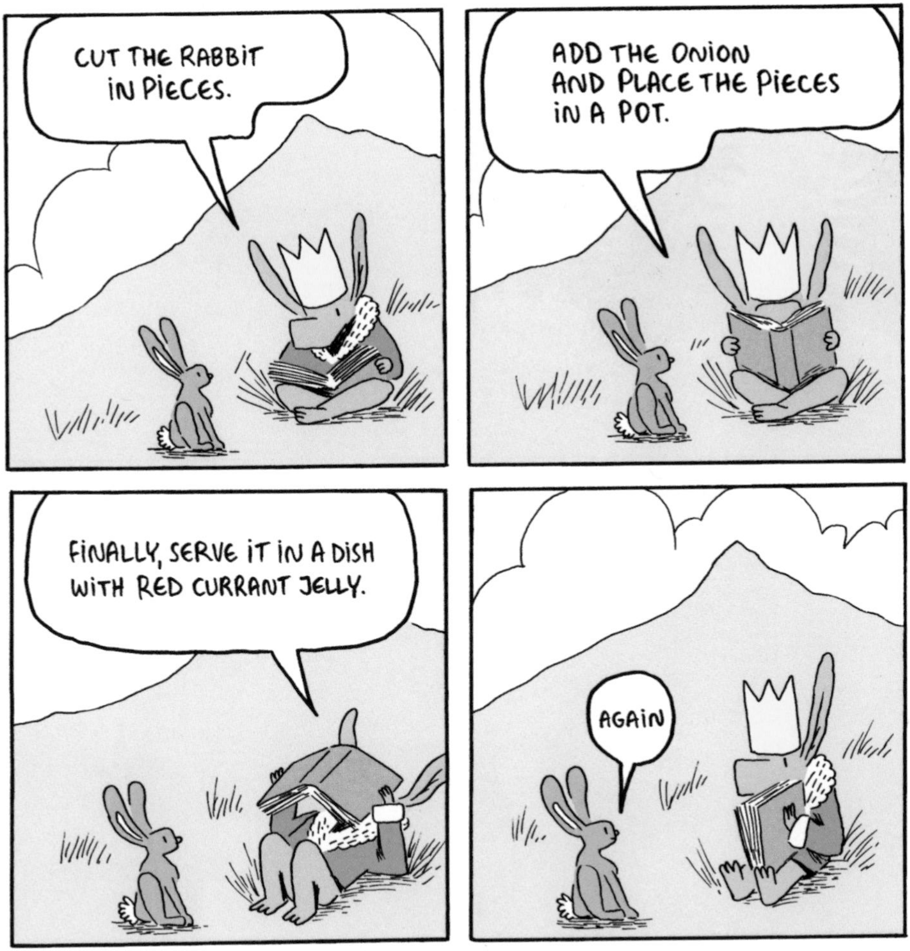
CUT THE RABBIT IN PIECES.
ADD THE ONION AND PLACE THE PIECES IN A POT.
FINALLY, SERVE IT IN A DISH WITH RED CURRANT JELLY.
AGAIN

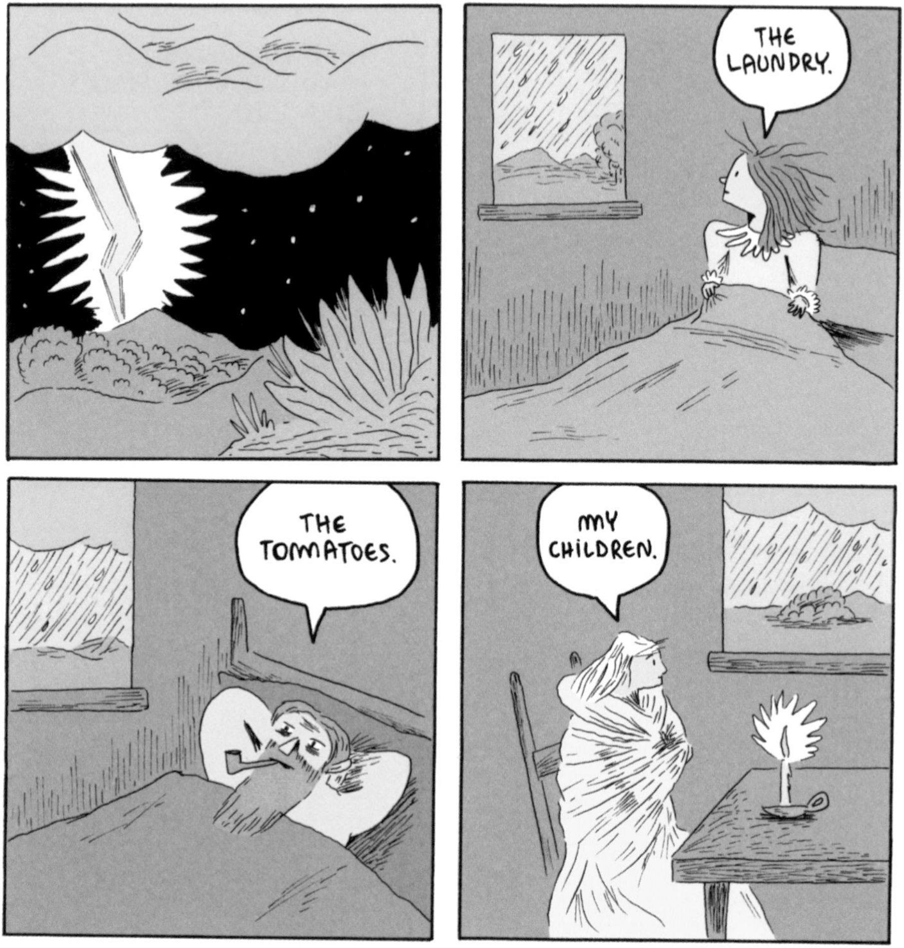
THE LAUNDRY.
THE TOMATOES.
MY CHILDREN.

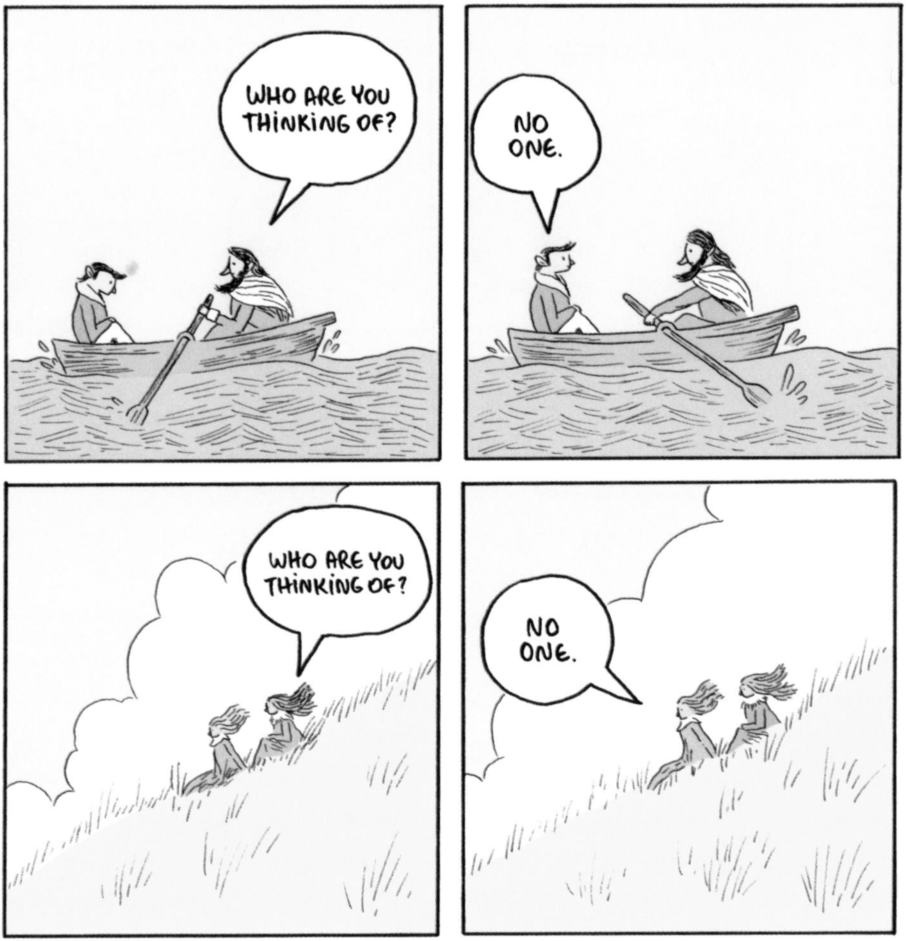
WHO ARE YOU THINKING OF?
NO ONE.
WHO ARE YOU THINKING OF?
NO ONE.

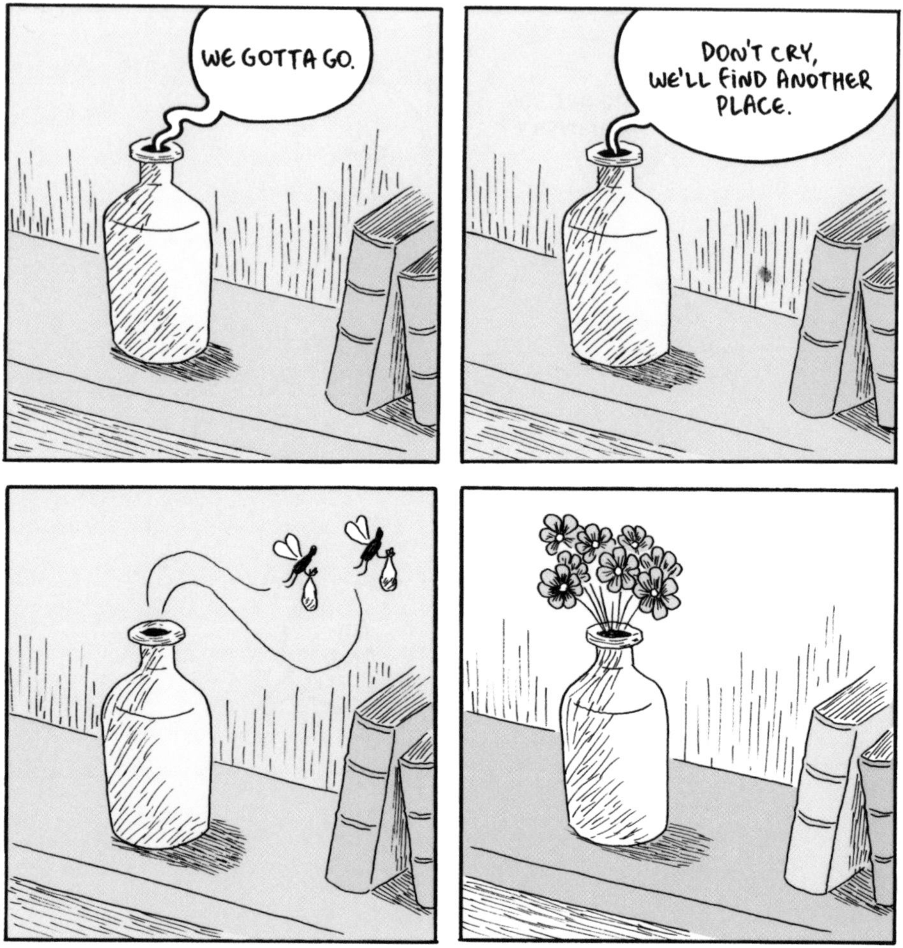
WE GOTTA GO.
DON'T CRY, WE'LL FIND ANOTHER PLACE.

!
IT'S A MAIDEN!

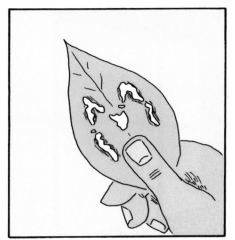

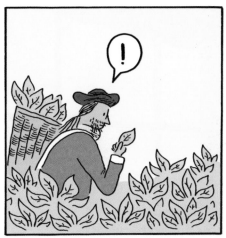

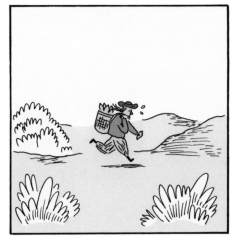

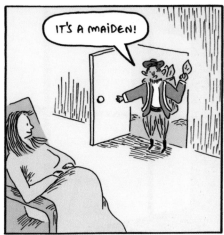

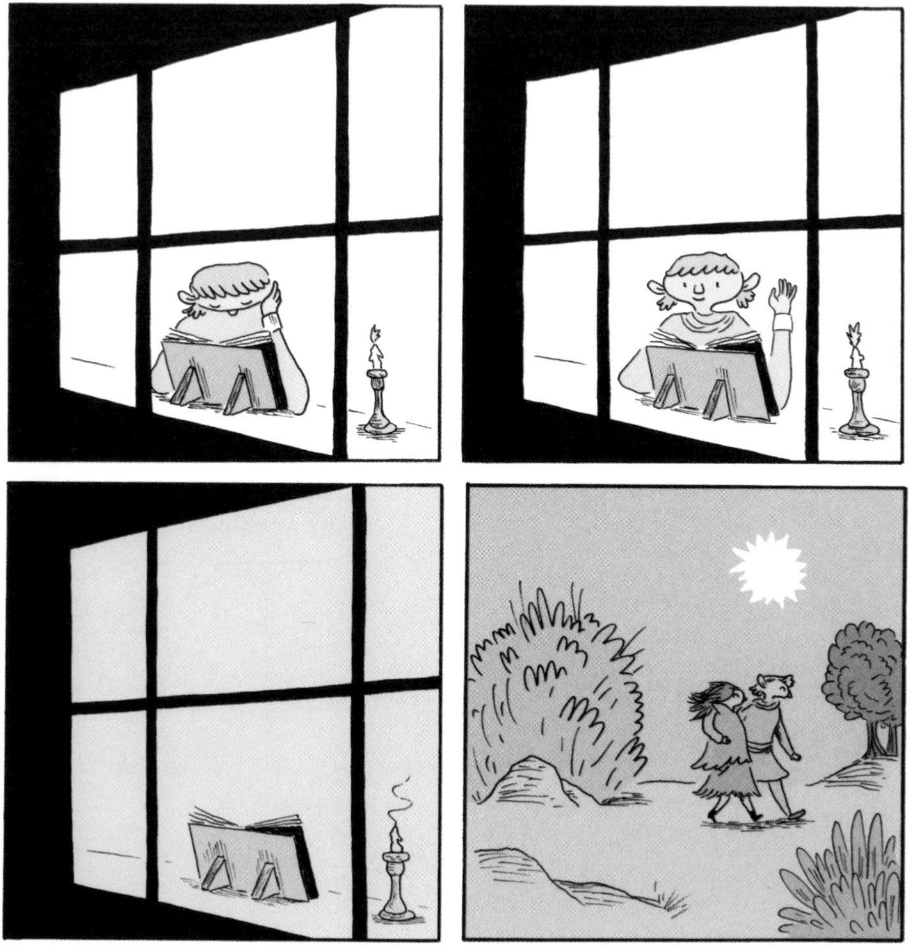

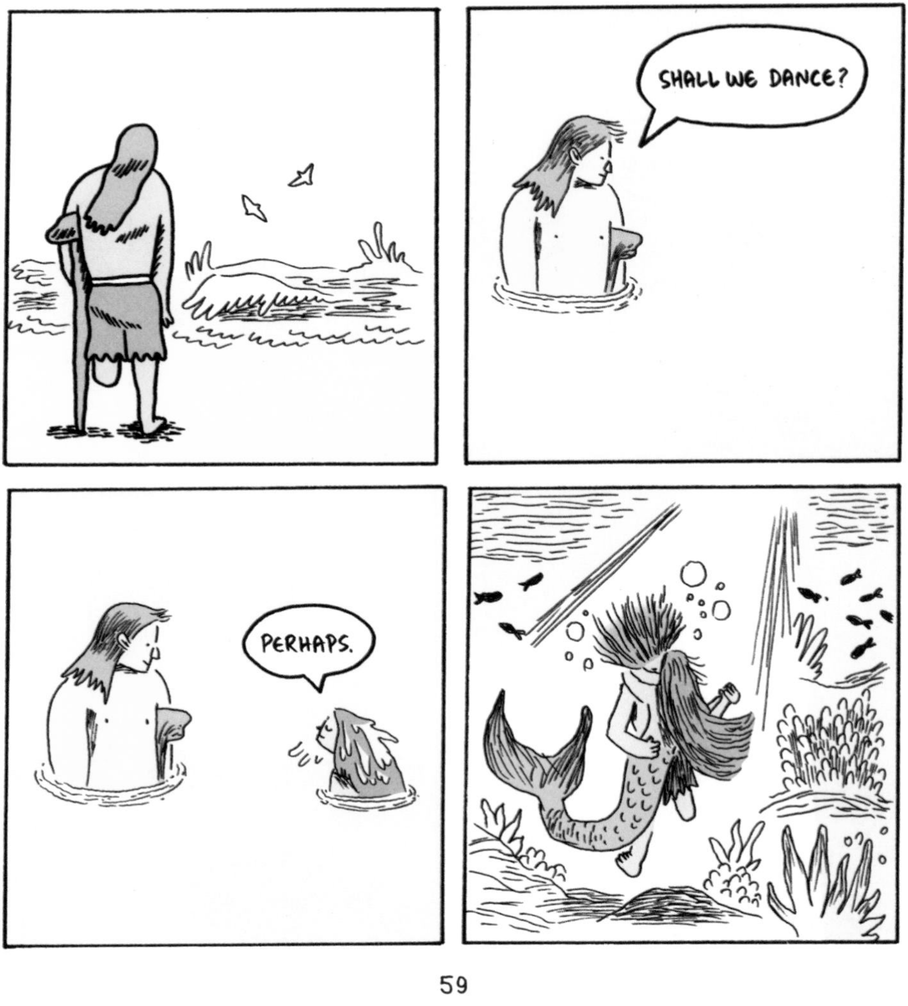
SHALL WE DANCE?
PERHAPS.

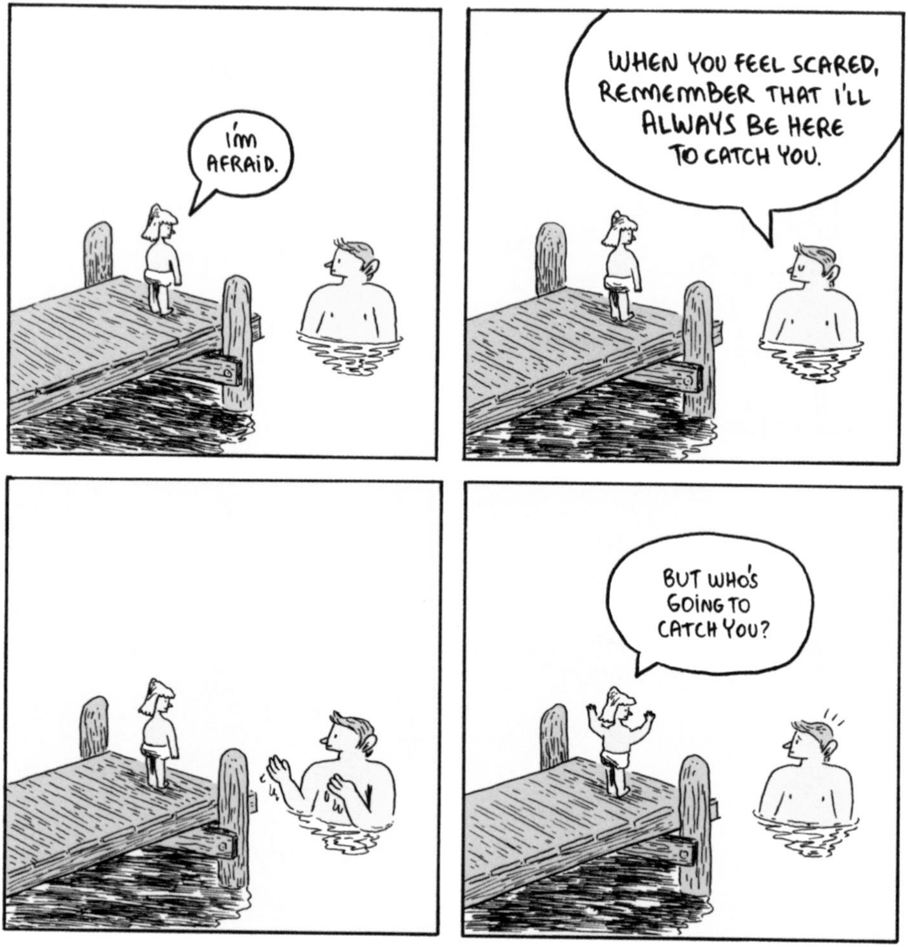
I'M AFRAID.
WHEN YOU FEEL SCARED, REMEMBER THAT I'LL ALWAYS BE HERE TO CATCH YOU.
BUT WHO'S GOING TO CATCH YOU?

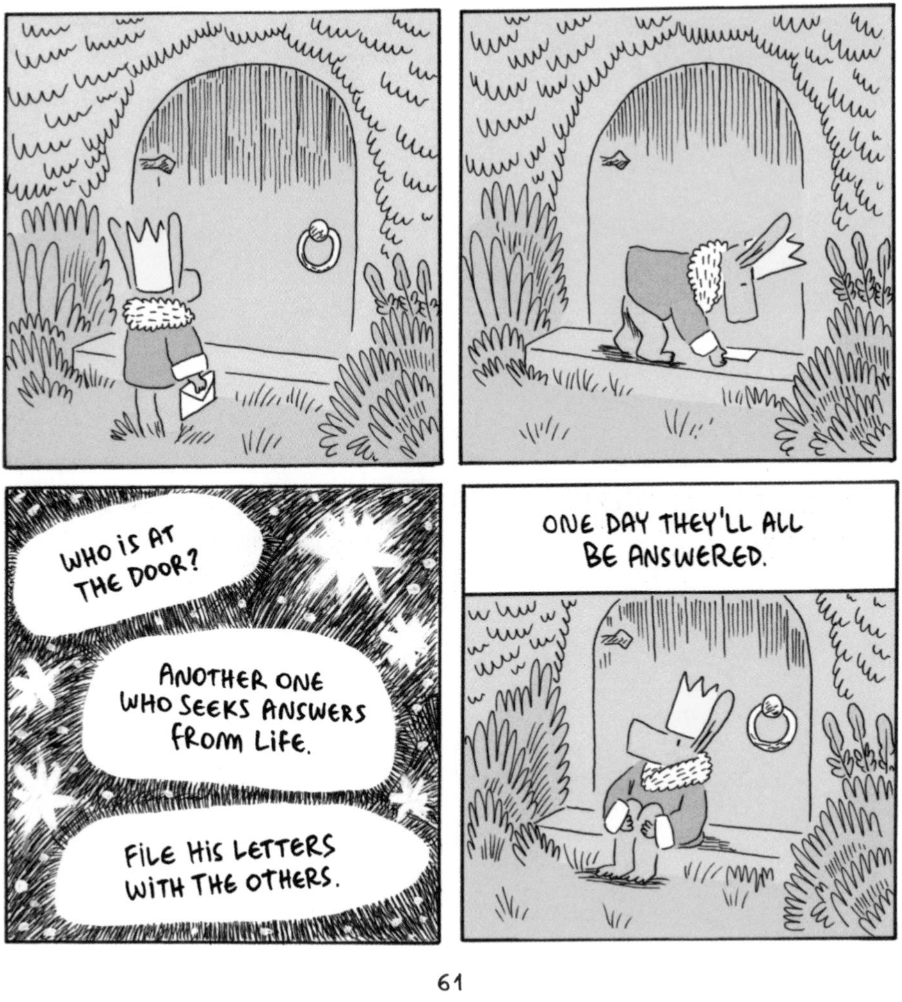
WHO IS AT THE DOOR?
ANOTHER ONE WHO SEEKS ANSWERS FROM LIFE.
FILE HIS LETTERS WITH THE OTHERS.
ONE DAY THEY'LL ALL BE ANSWERED.

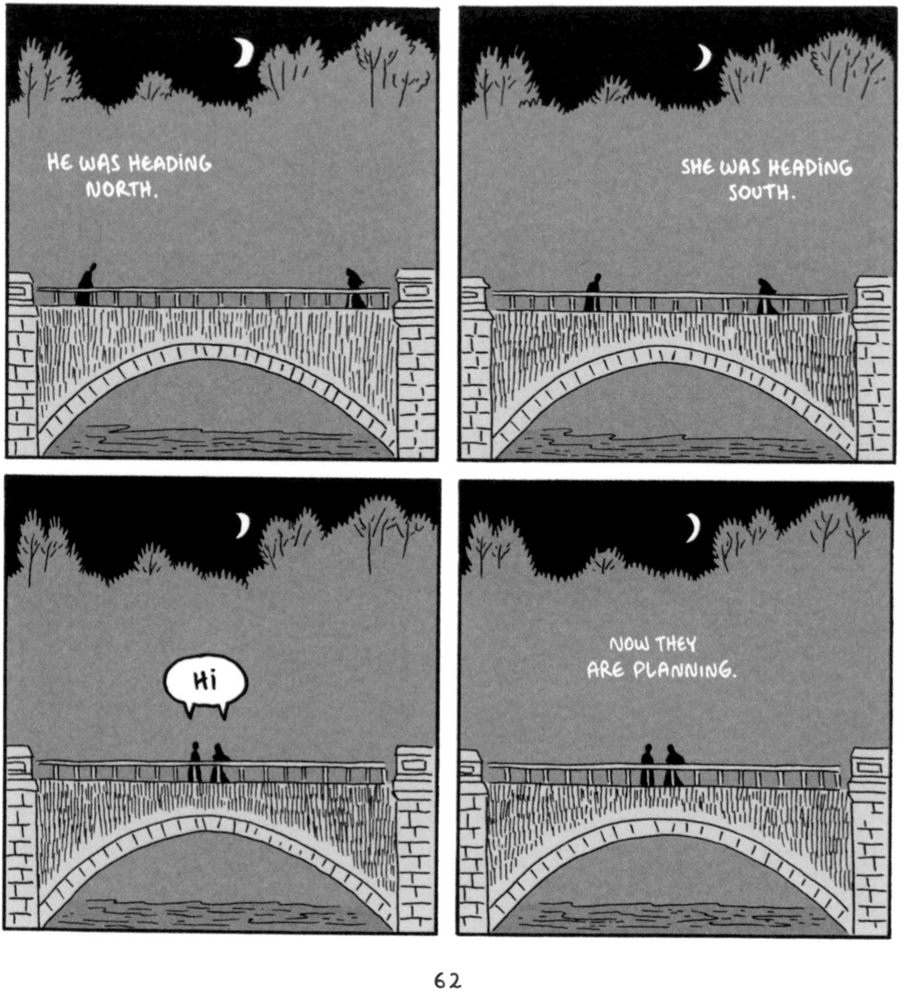
HE WAS HEADING NORTH.
SHE WAS HEADING SOUTH.
Hi
NOW THEY ARE PLANNING.

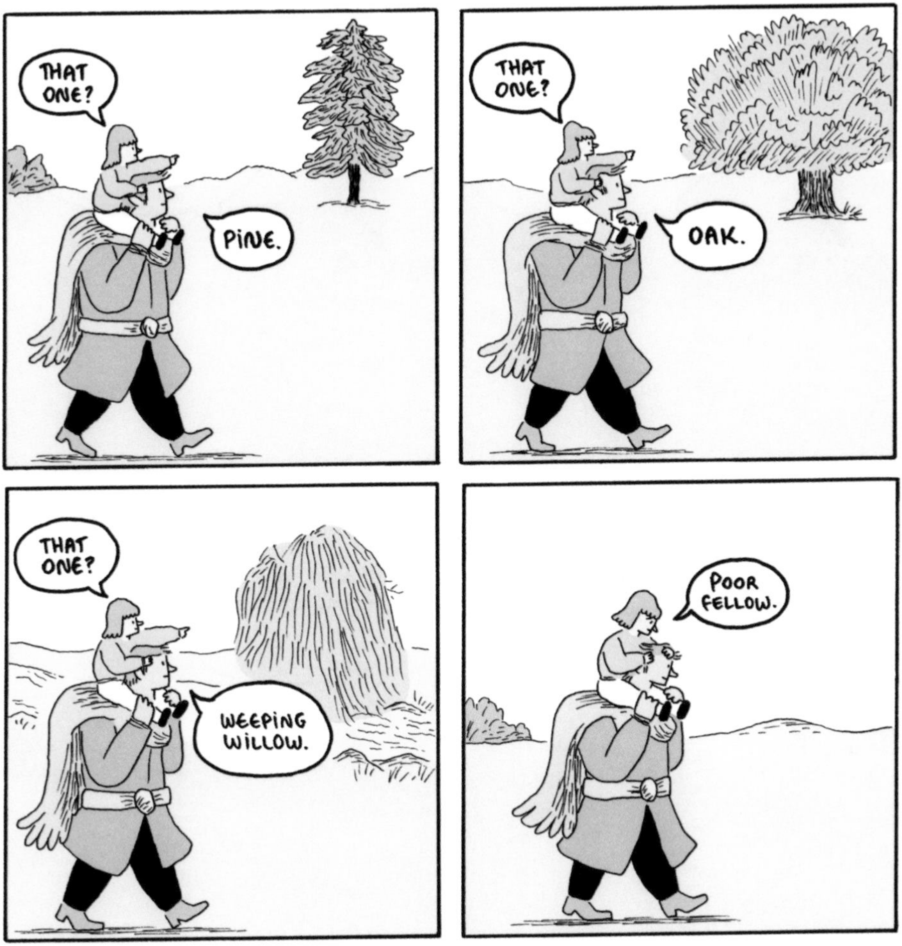
THAT ONE?
PINE.
THAT ONE?
OAK.
THAT ONE?
WEEPING WILLOW.
POOR FELLOW.

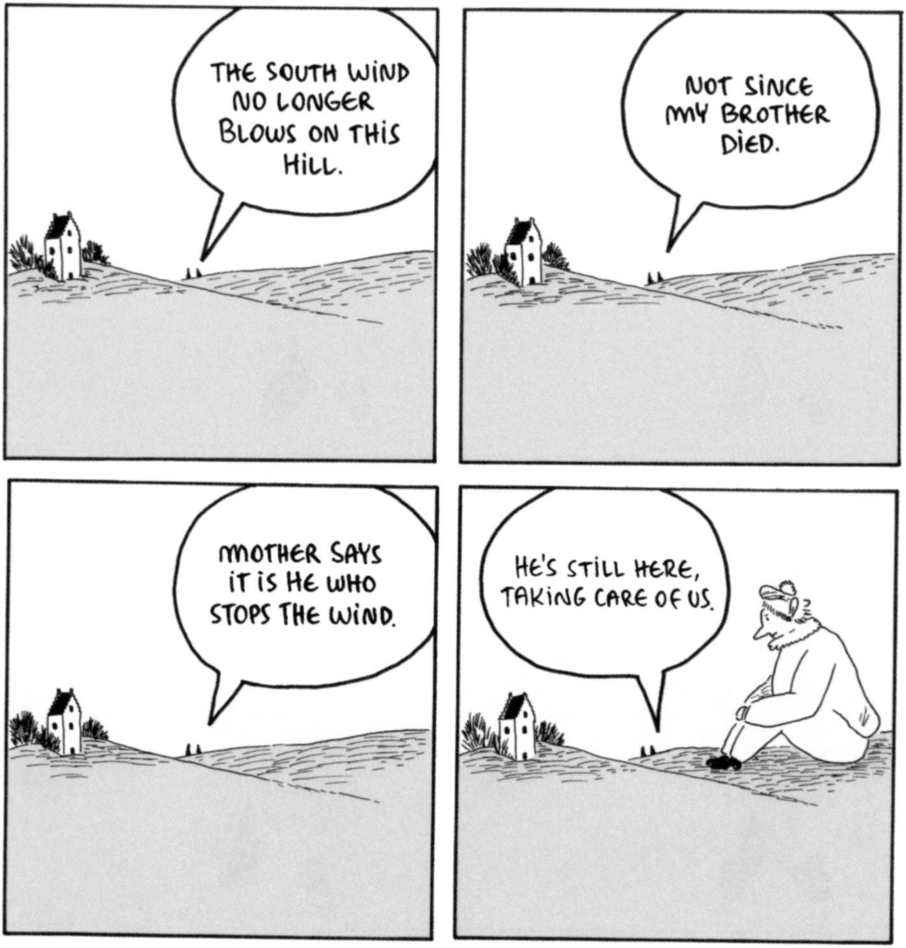
THE SOUTH WIND NO LONGER BLOWS ON THIS HILL.
NOT SINCE MY BROTHER DIED.
MOTHER SAYS IT IS HE WHO STOPS THE WIND.
HE'S STILL HERE, TAKING CARE OF US.

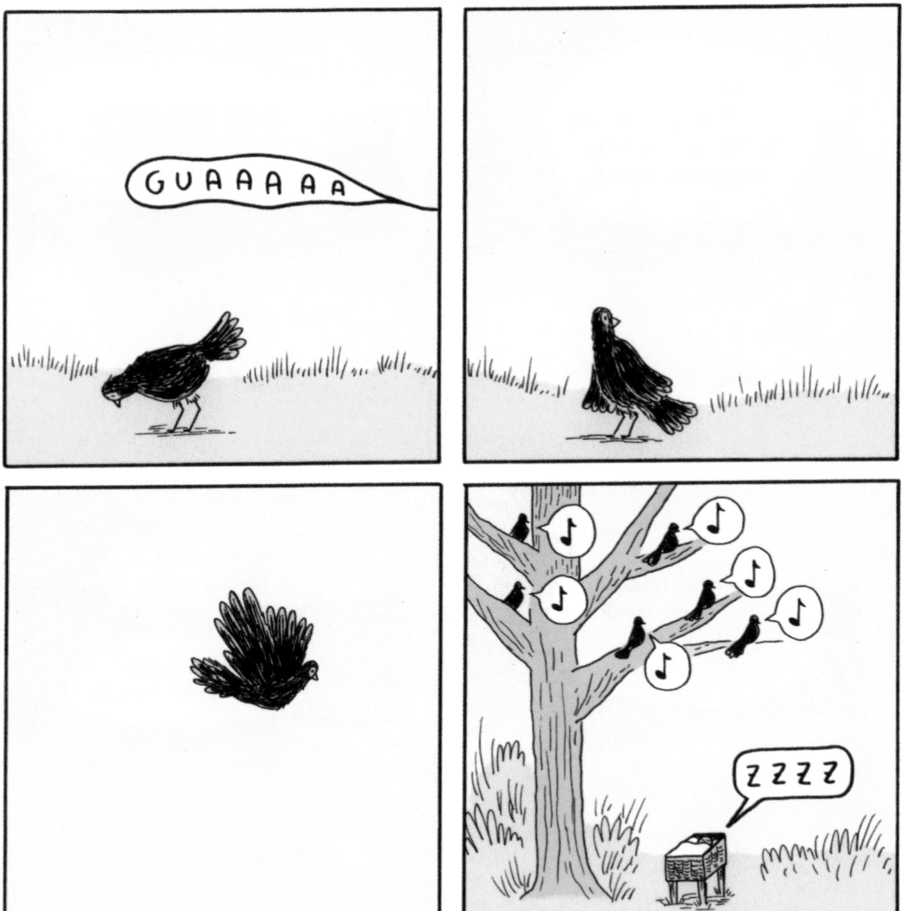
GUAAAAA
♪
♪
♪
♪
♪
♪
♪
ZZZZ

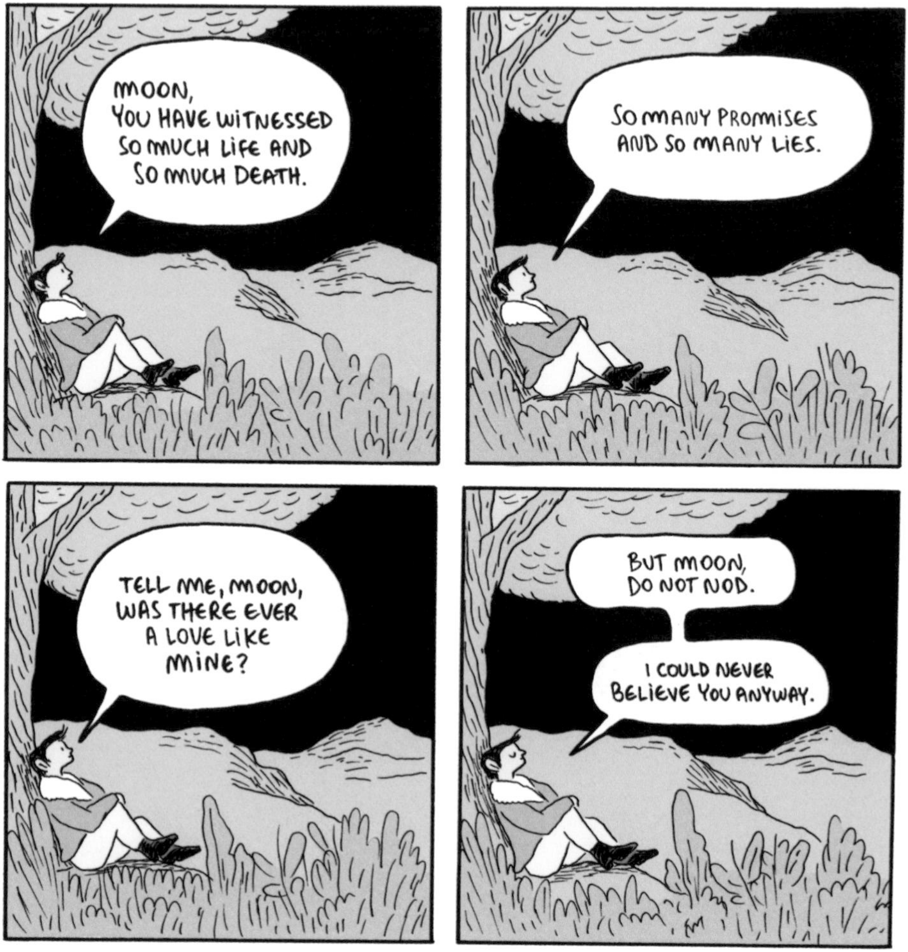
MOON,
YOU HAVE WITNESSED
SO MUCH LIFE AND
SO MUCH DEATH.
SO MANY PROMISES
AND SO MANY LIES.
TELL ME, MOON,
WAS THERE EVER
A LOVE LIKE
MINE?
BUT MOON,
DO NOT NOD.
I COULD NEVER
BELIEVE YOU ANYWAY.

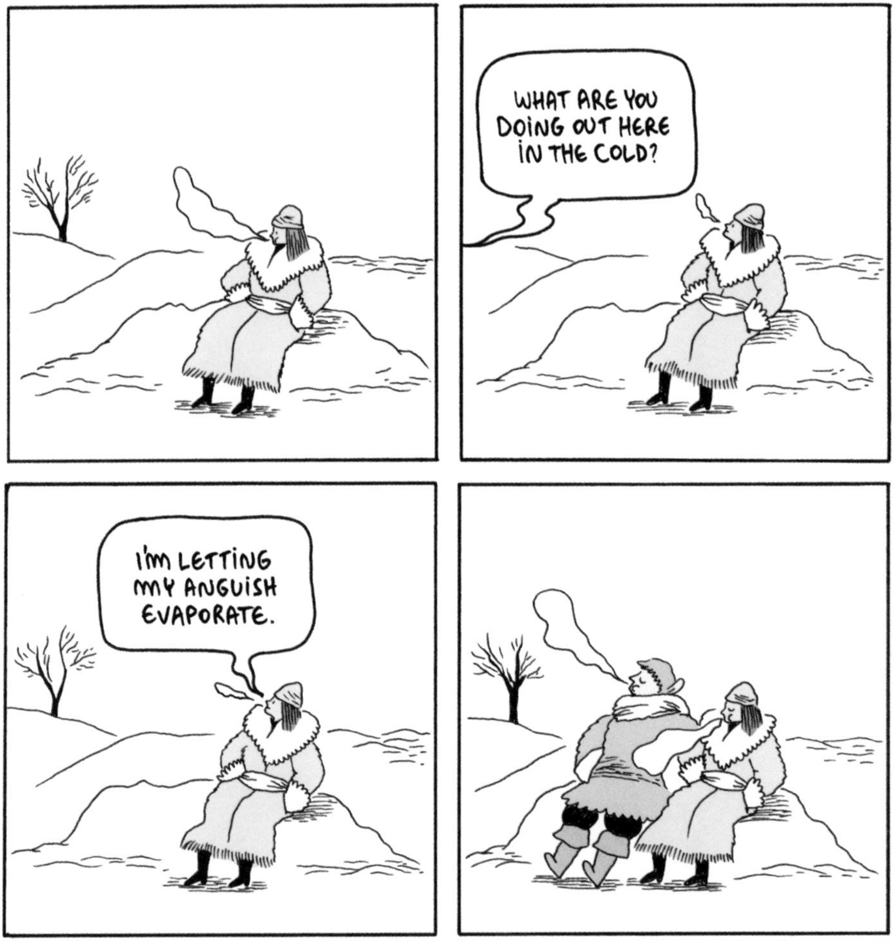
WHAT ARE YOU DOING OUT HERE IN THE COLD?
I'M LETTING MY ANGUISH EVAPORATE.

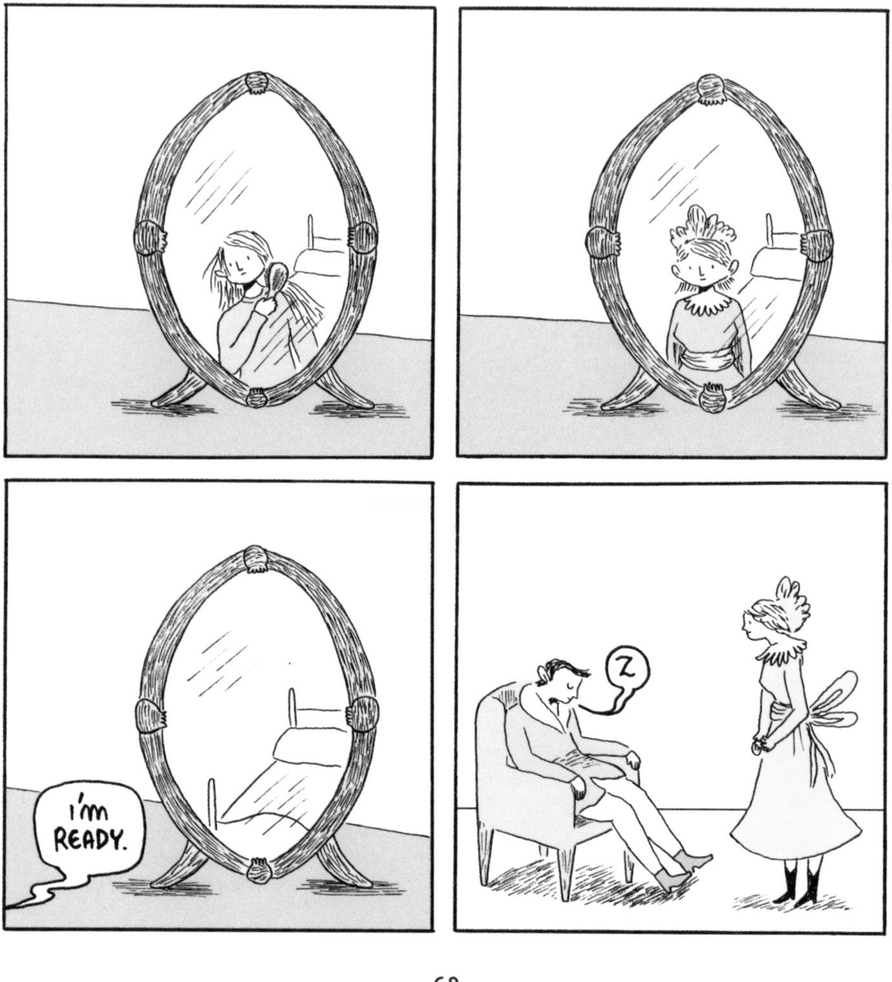
I'M READY.
Z

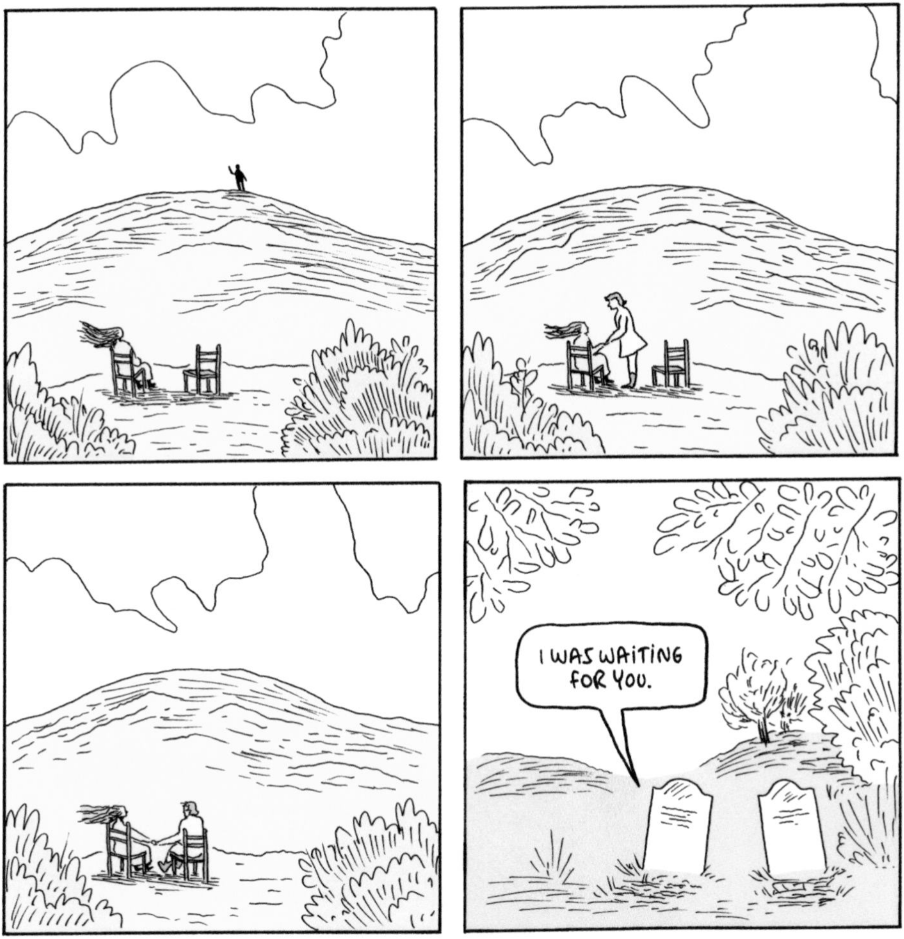
I WAS WAITING FOR YOU.

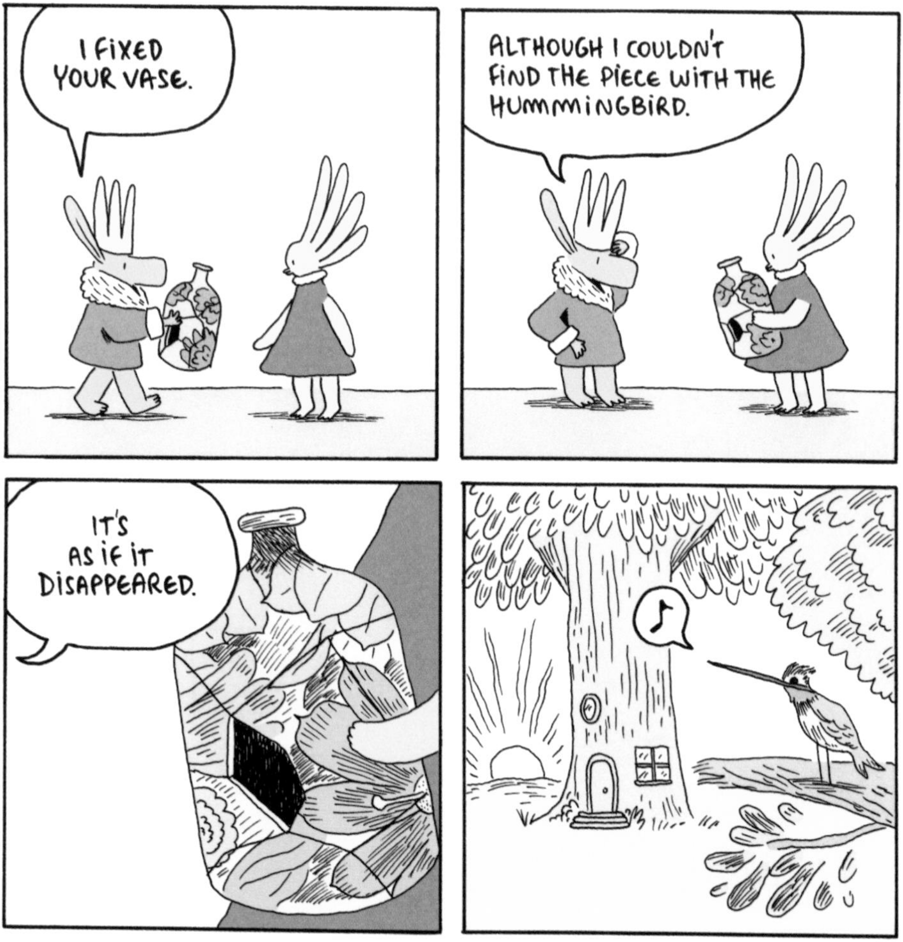
I FIXED YOUR VASE.
ALTHOUGH I COULDN'T FIND THE PIECE WITH THE HUMMINGBIRD.
IT'S AS IF IT DISAPPEARED.

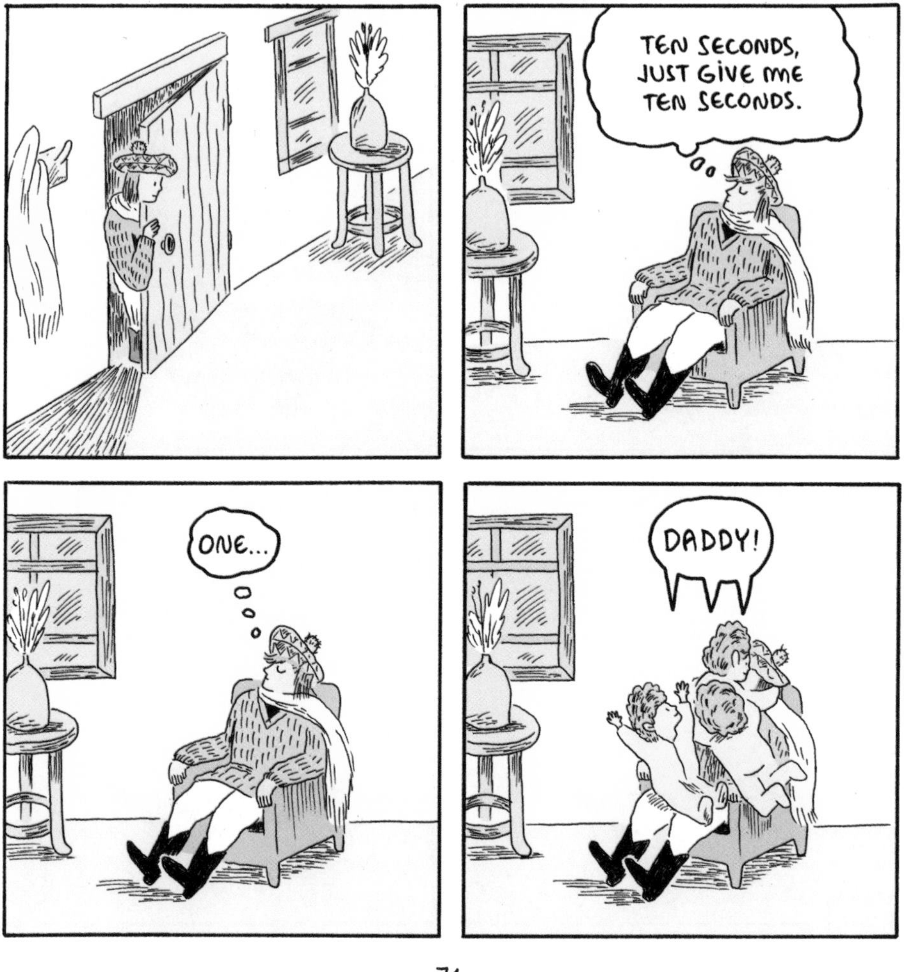
TEN SECONDS,
JUST GIVE ME
TEN SECONDS.
ONE...
DADDY!

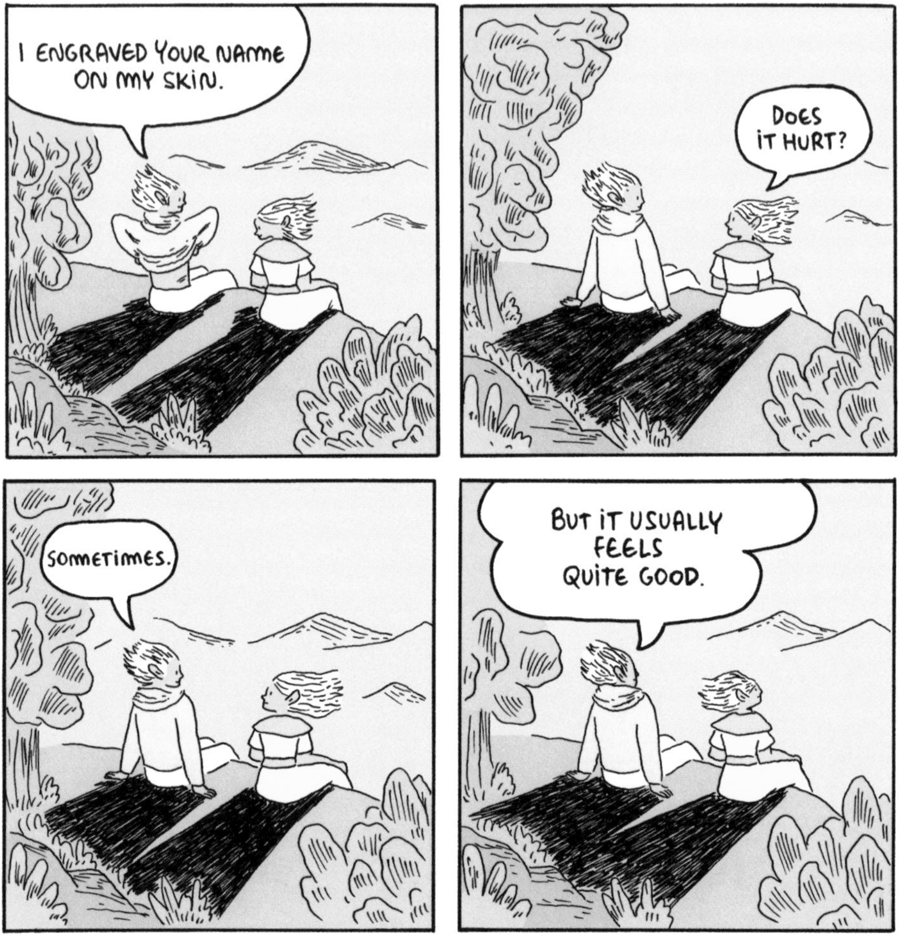
I ENGRAVED YOUR NAME ON MY SKIN.
DOES IT HURT?
SOMETIMES.
BUT IT USUALLY FEELS QUITE GOOD.

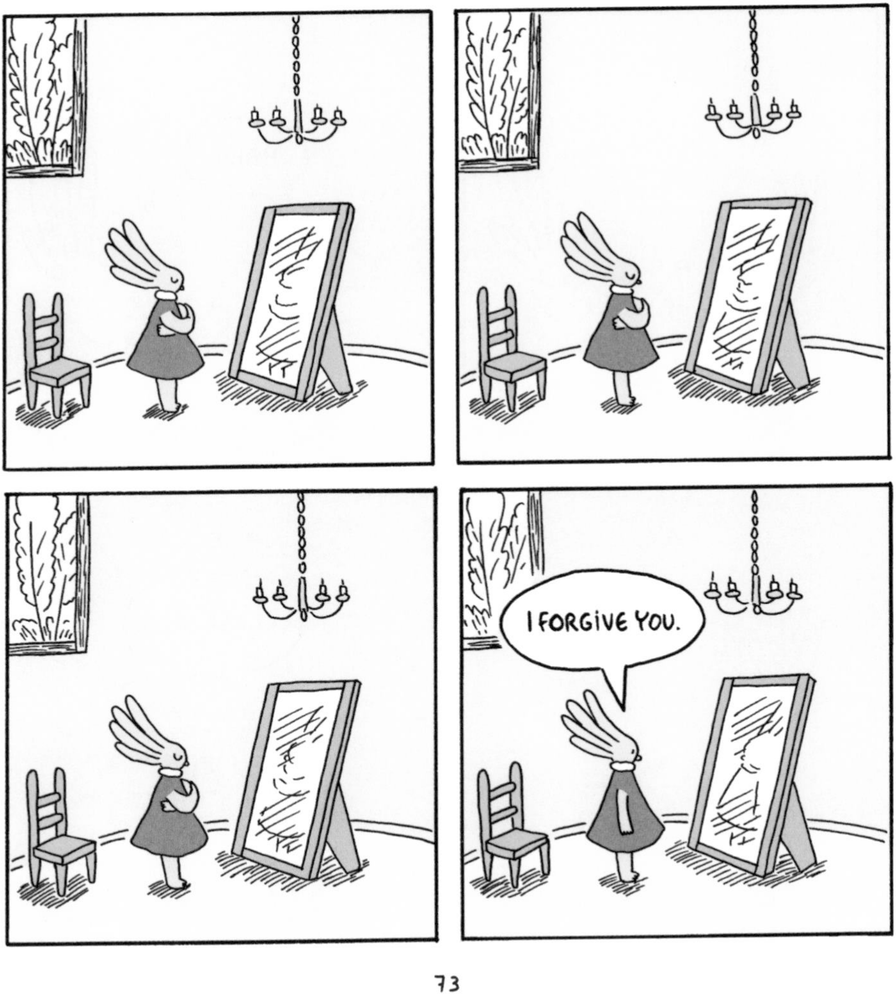
I FORGIVE YOU.

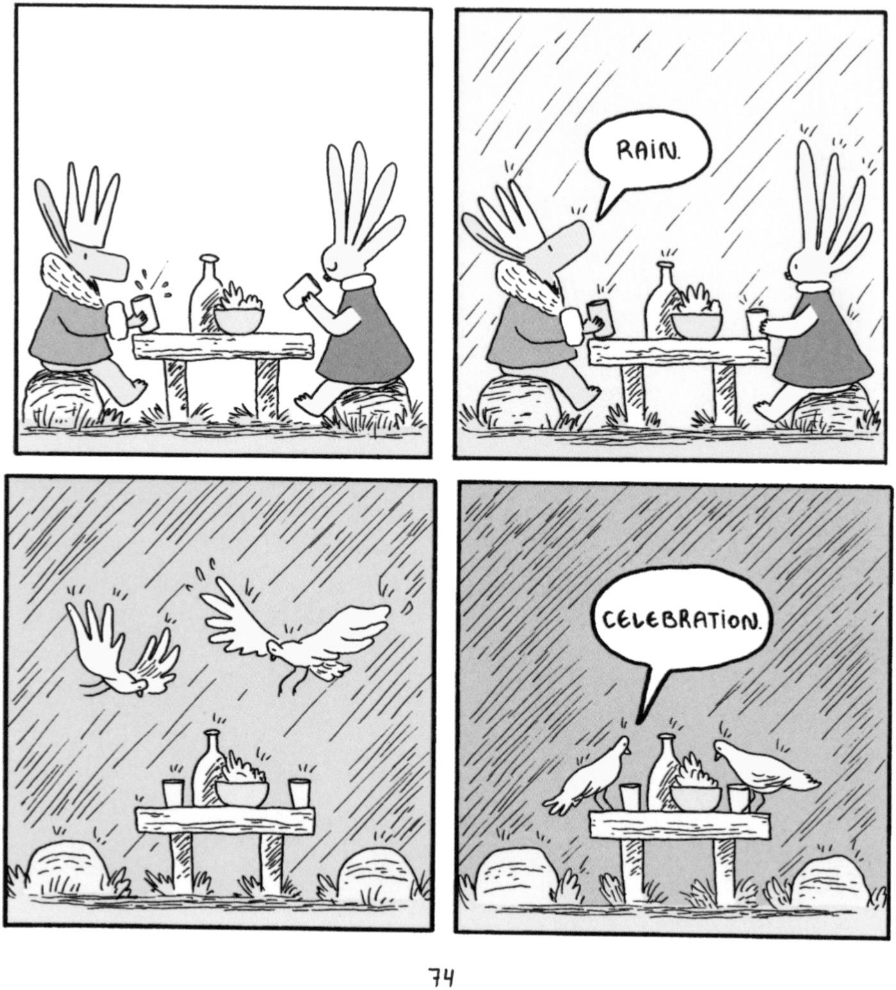
RAIN.
CELEBRATION.

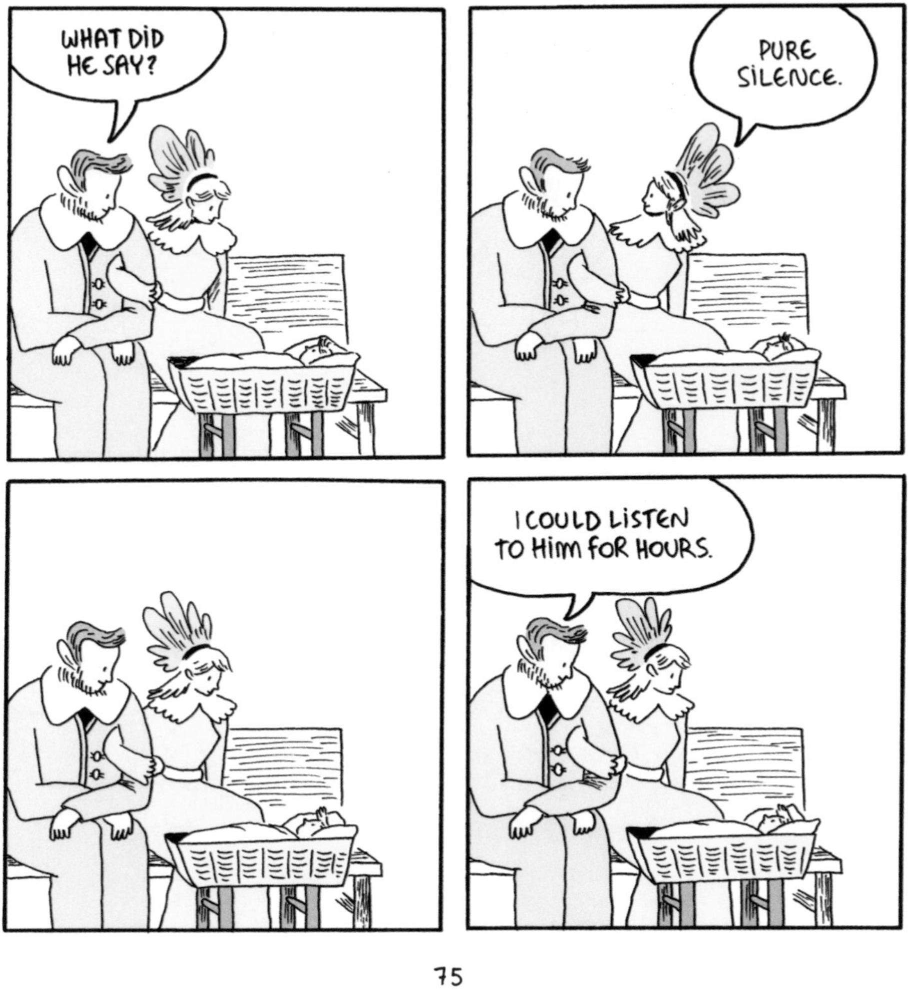
WHAT DID HE SAY?
PURE SILENCE.
I COULD LISTEN TO HIM FOR HOURS.

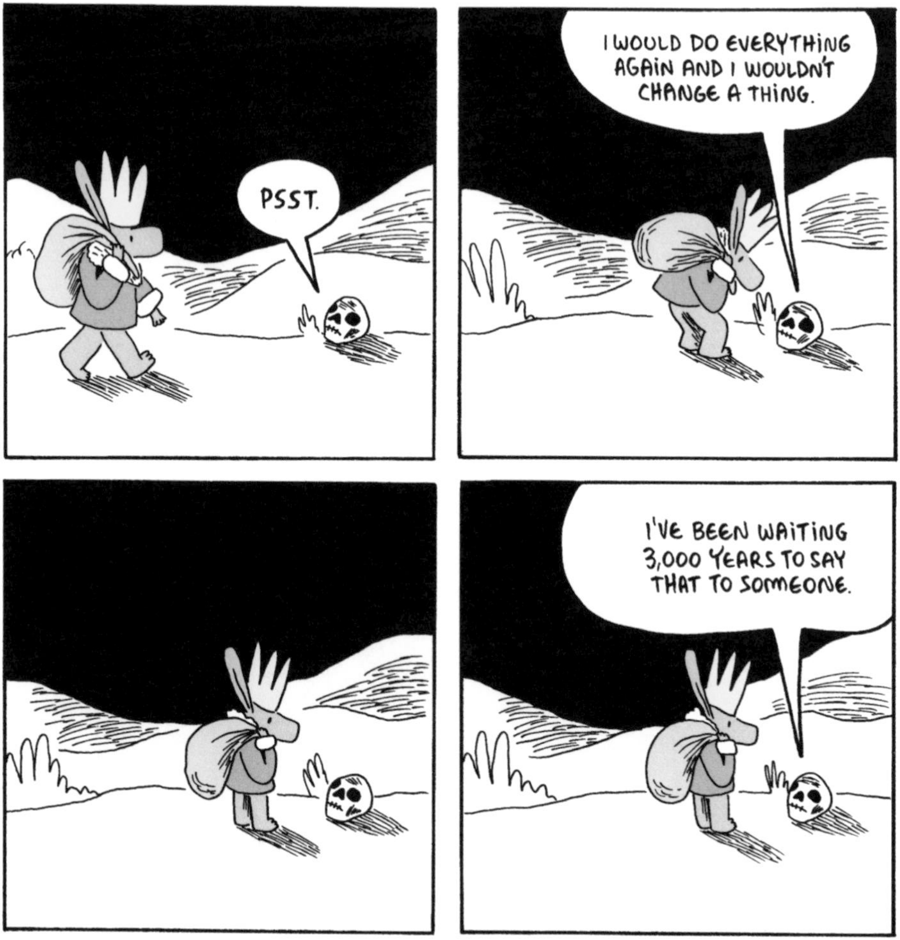
PSST.
I WOULD DO EVERYTHING AGAIN AND I WOULDN'T CHANGE A THING.
I'VE BEEN WAITING 3,000 YEARS TO SAY THAT TO SOMEONE.

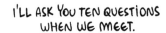

I'LL ASK YOU TEN QUESTIONS WHEN WE MEET.

ONE ABOUT LAUGHTER AND MOUNTAINS.

ONE ABOUT ROCKS AND AGONY.

ONE ABOUT MUSIC AND WIND.

AND SEVEN ABOUT WOMAN AND HER MYSTERIES.

77

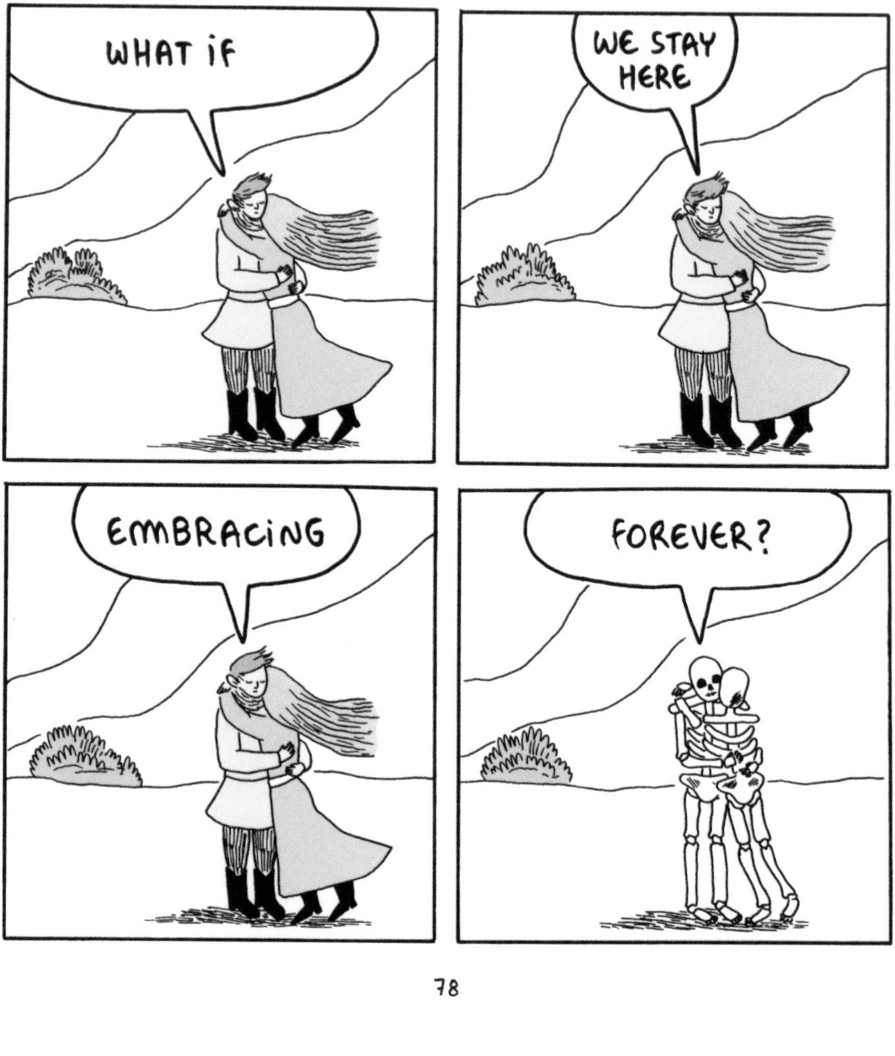
WHAT IF
WE STAY HERE
EMBRACING
FOREVER?

ONE MORE STAR REVOLVES CONSTANTLY AROUND THE PLANET.
SUDDENLY, A SMALL REVOLUTIONARY ACT LIBERATES IT FROM THIS MAD RACE.
NOW, DON'T RUN ANYMORE.
SO MUCH HAPPINESS MAKES IT BURST INTO A SUPERNOVA
THAT INUNDATES THE ENTIRE UNIVERSE WITH A NECESSARY ENERGY.
I'M TIRED OF THIS JOB.

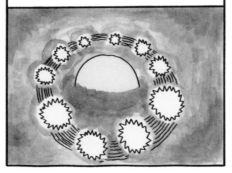

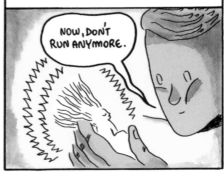

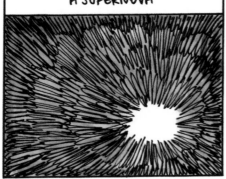

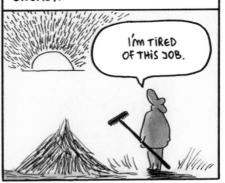

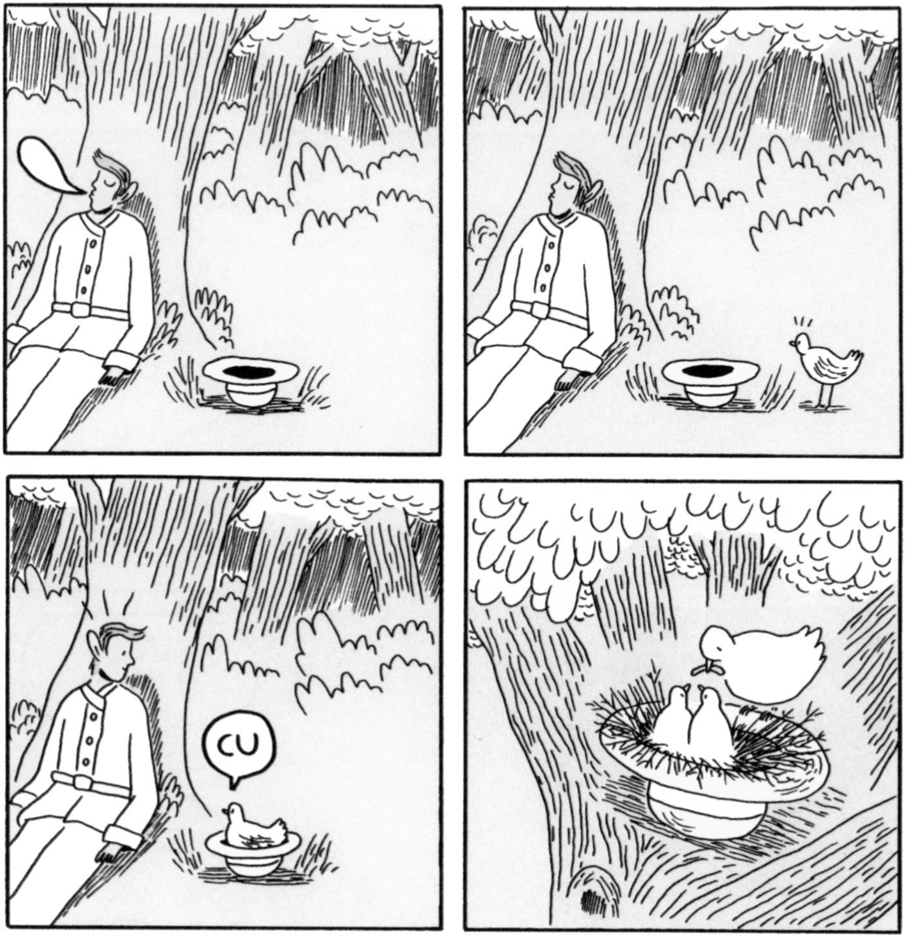
CU

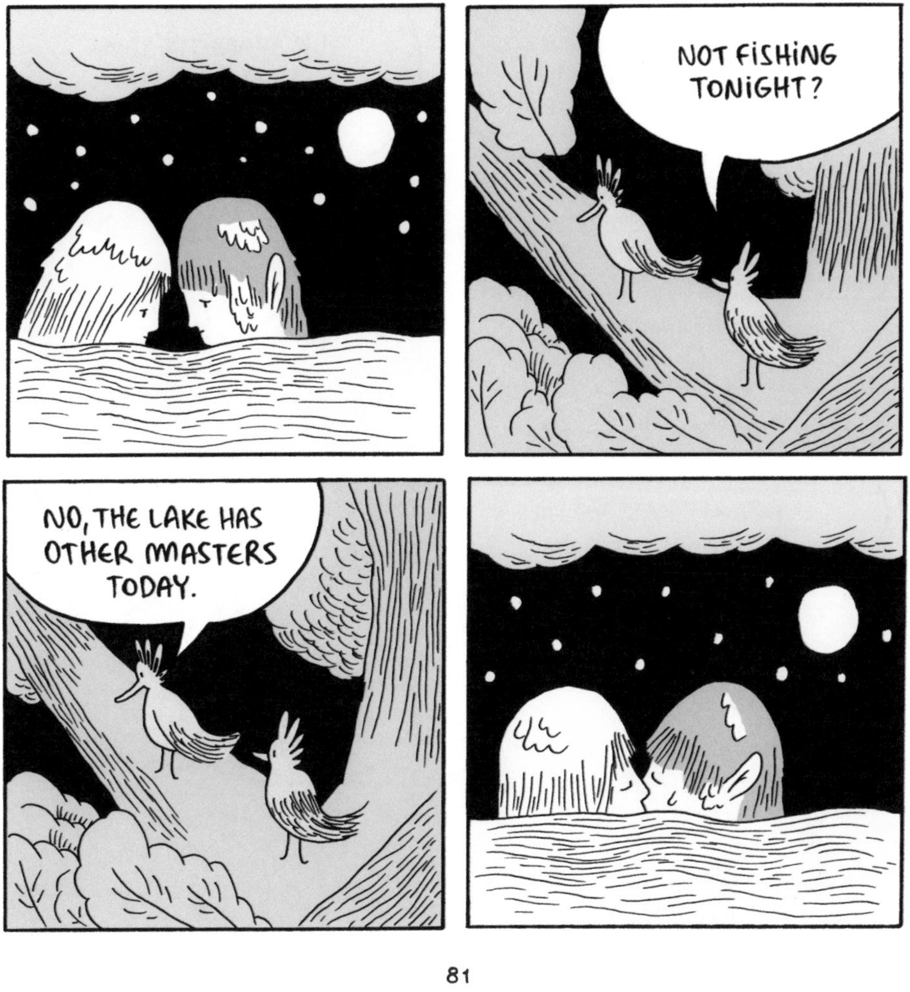
NOT FISHING TONIGHT?
NO, THE LAKE HAS OTHER MASTERS TODAY.

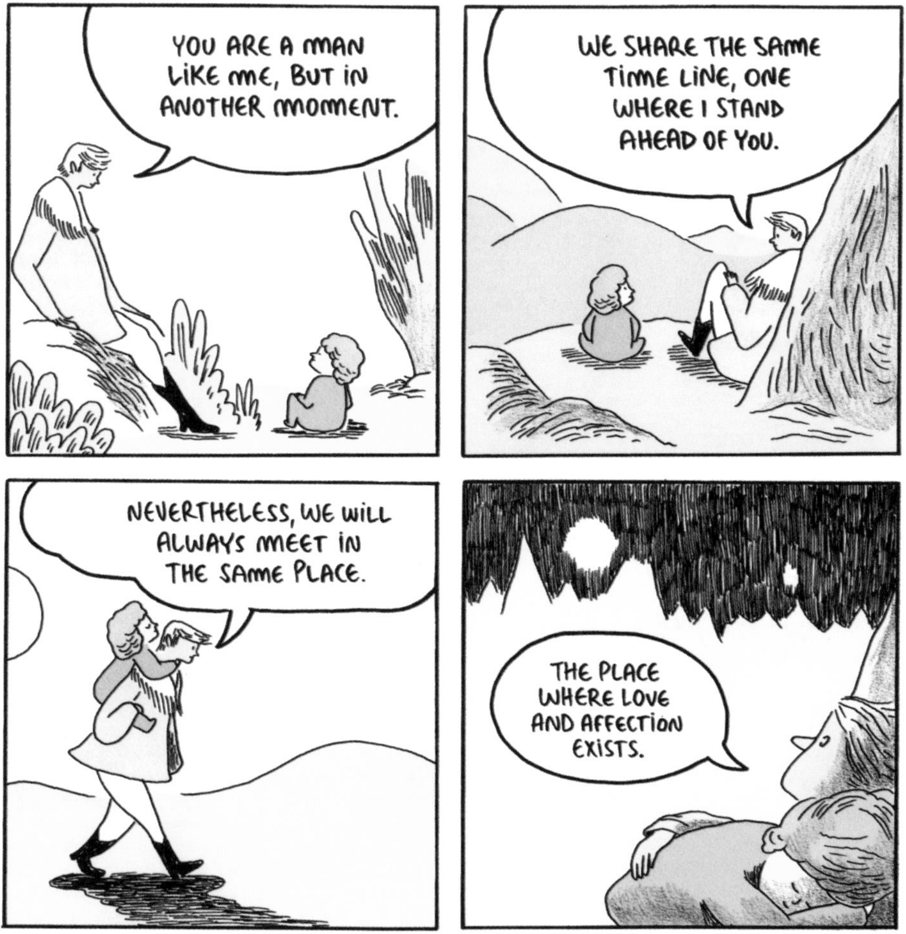
YOU ARE A MAN LIKE ME, BUT IN ANOTHER MOMENT.
WE SHARE THE SAME TIME LINE, ONE WHERE I STAND AHEAD OF YOU.
NEVERTHELESS, WE WILL ALWAYS MEET IN THE SAME PLACE.
THE PLACE WHERE LOVE AND AFFECTION EXISTS.

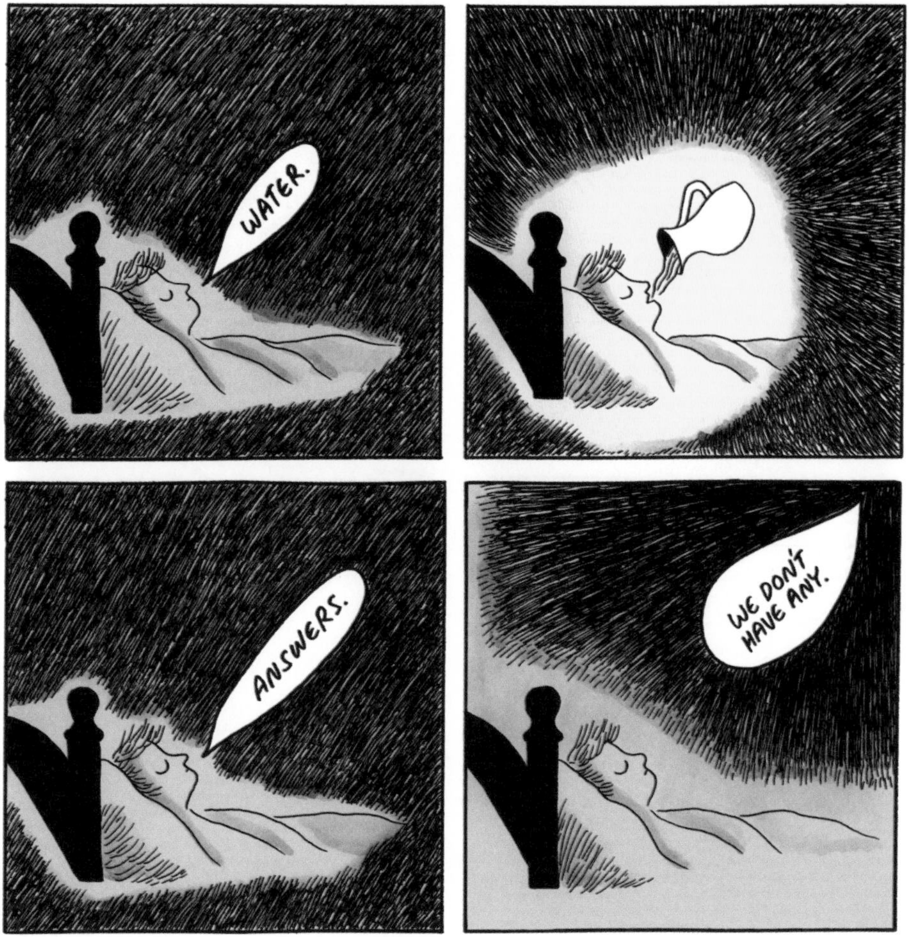
WATER.
ANSWERS.
WE DON'T HAVE ANY.

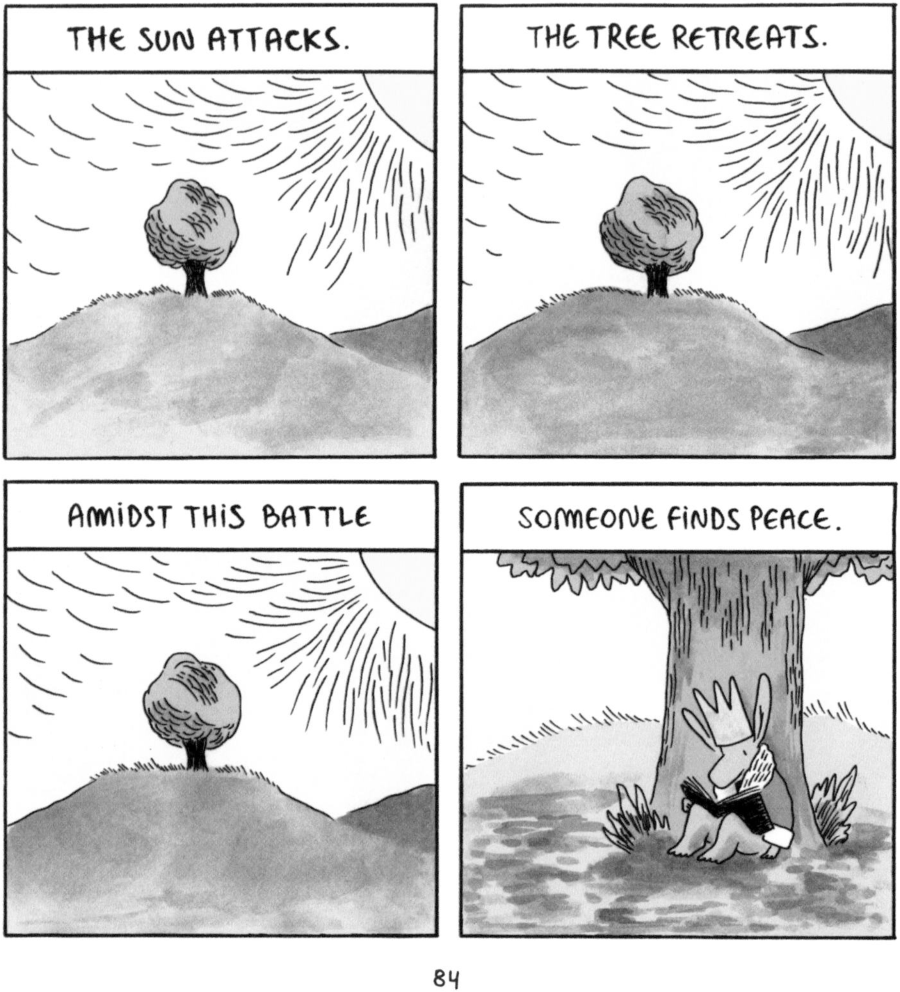
THE SUN ATTACKS.
THE TREE RETREATS.
AMIDST THIS BATTLE
SOMEONE FINDS PEACE.

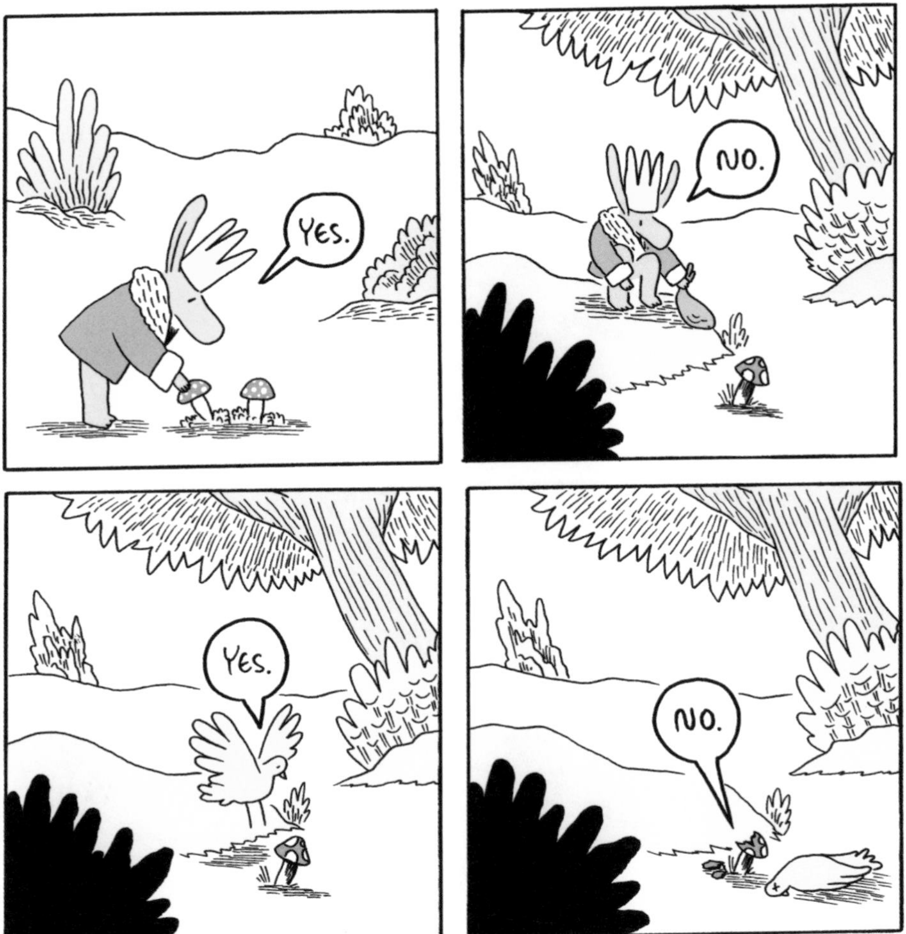
YES.
NO.
YES.
NO.

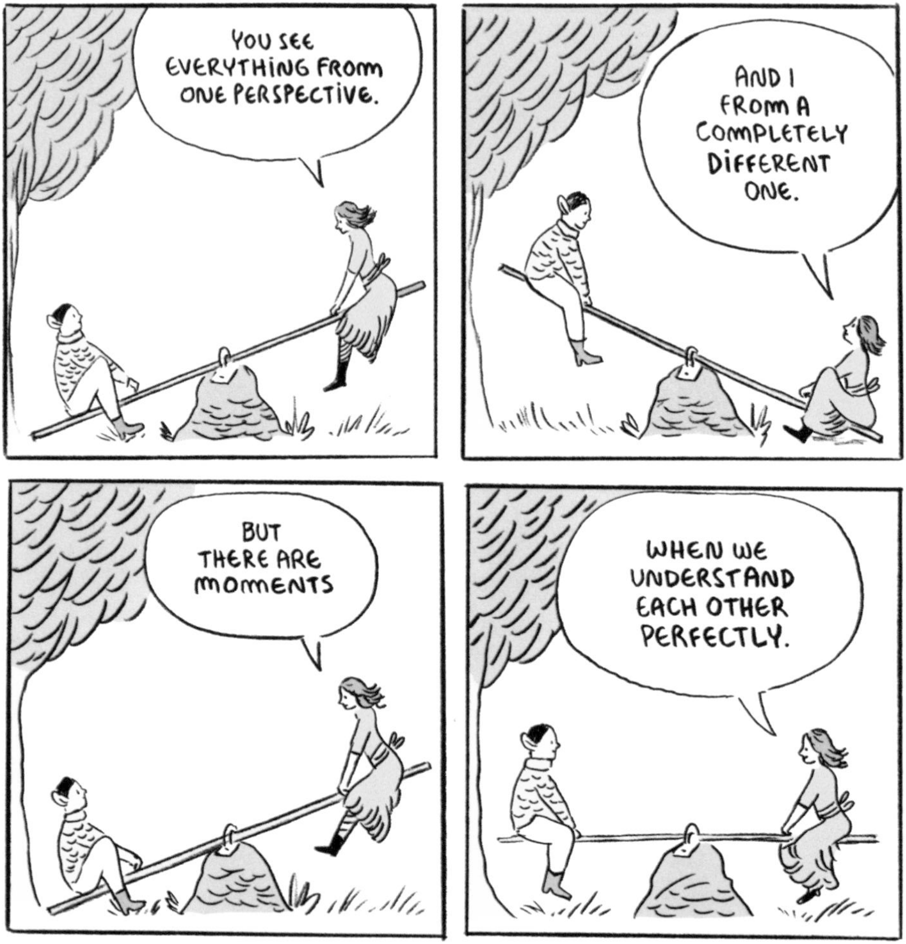
YOU SEE EVERYTHING FROM ONE PERSPECTIVE.
AND I FROM A COMPLETELY DIFFERENT ONE.
BUT THERE ARE MOMENTS
WHEN WE UNDERSTAND EACH OTHER PERFECTLY.

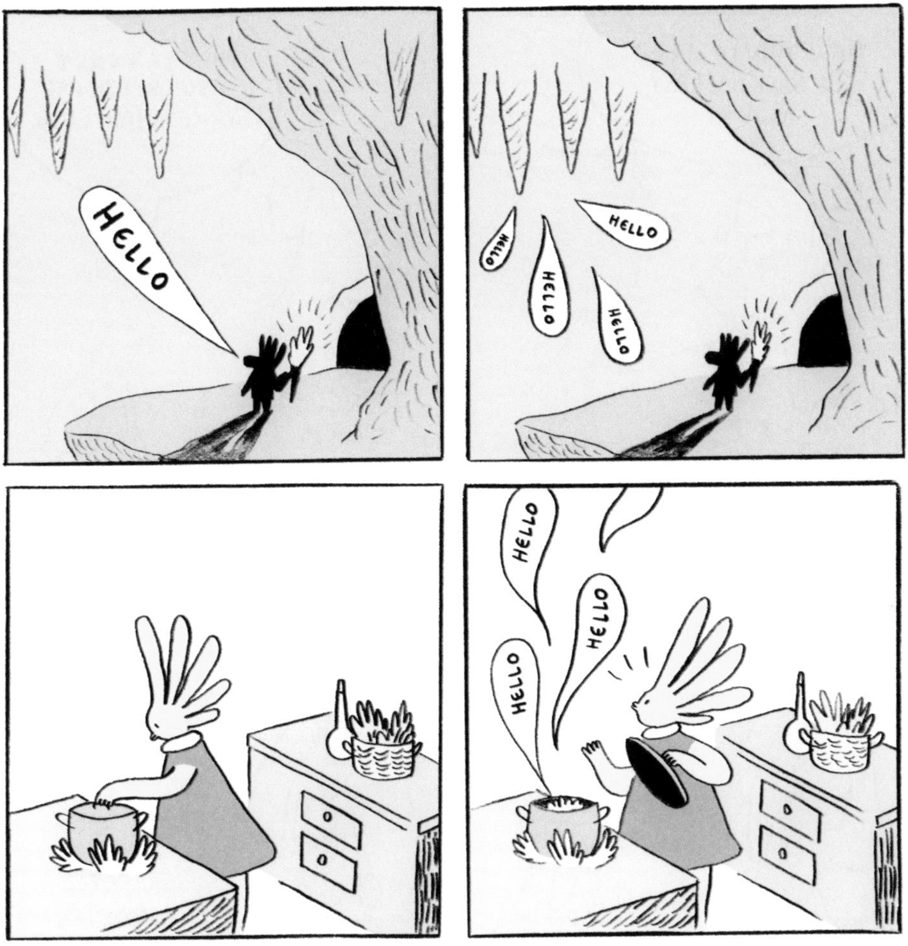
HELLO
HELLO
HELLO
HELLO
HELLO
HELLO
HELLO
HELLO

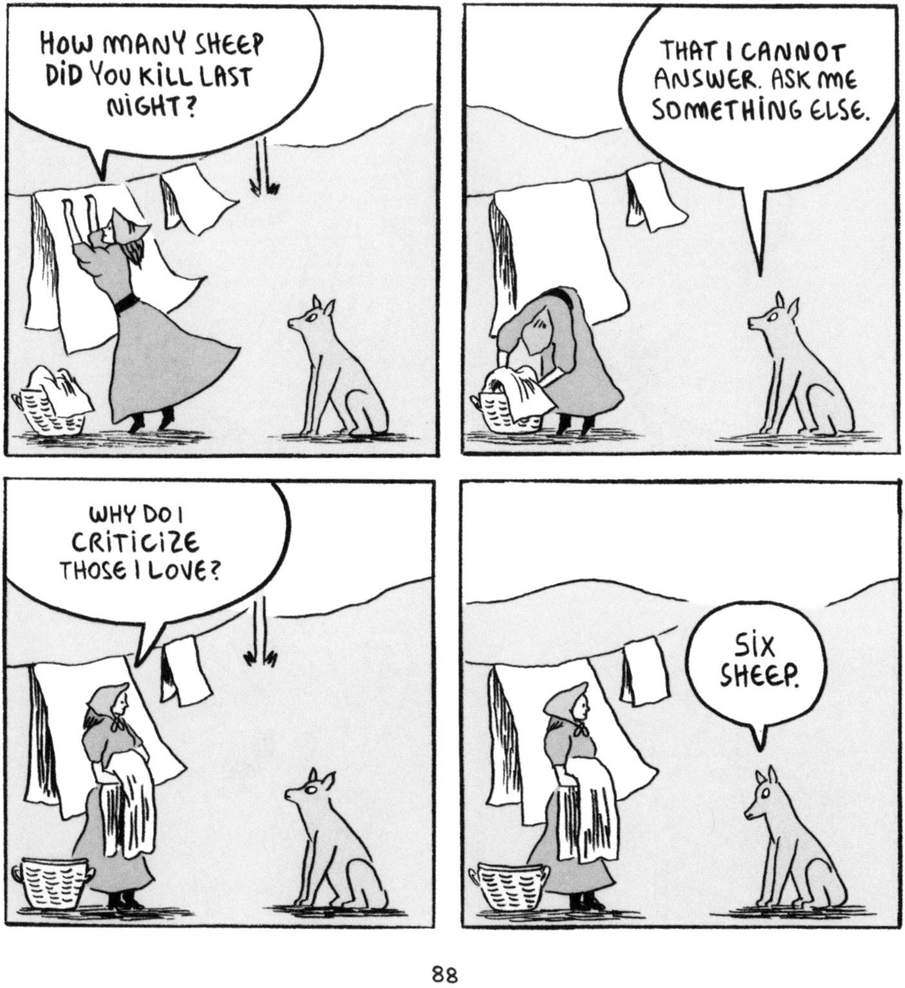
HOW MANY SHEEP DID YOU KILL LAST NIGHT?
THAT I CANNOT ANSWER. ASK ME SOMETHING ELSE.
WHY DO I CRITICIZE THOSE I LOVE?
SIX SHEEP.

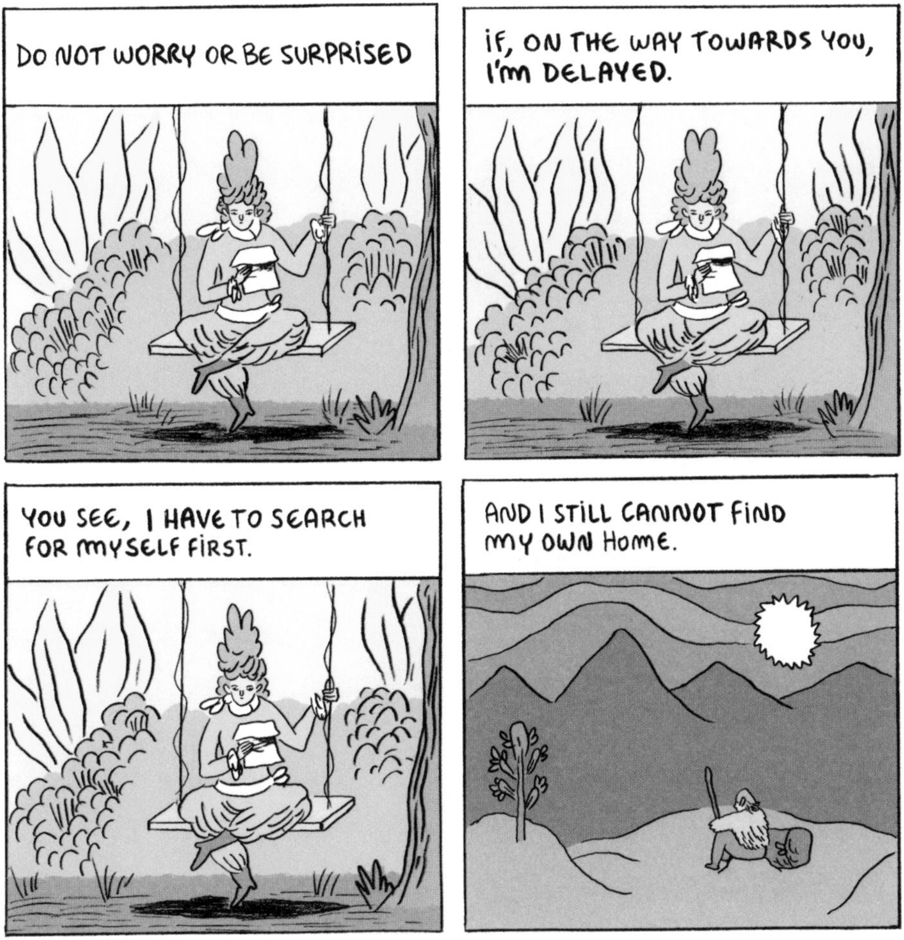
DO NOT WORRY OR BE SURPRISED
IF, ON THE WAY TOWARDS YOU, I'M DELAYED.
YOU SEE, I HAVE TO SEARCH FOR MYSELF FIRST.
AND I STILL CANNOT FIND MY OWN HOME.

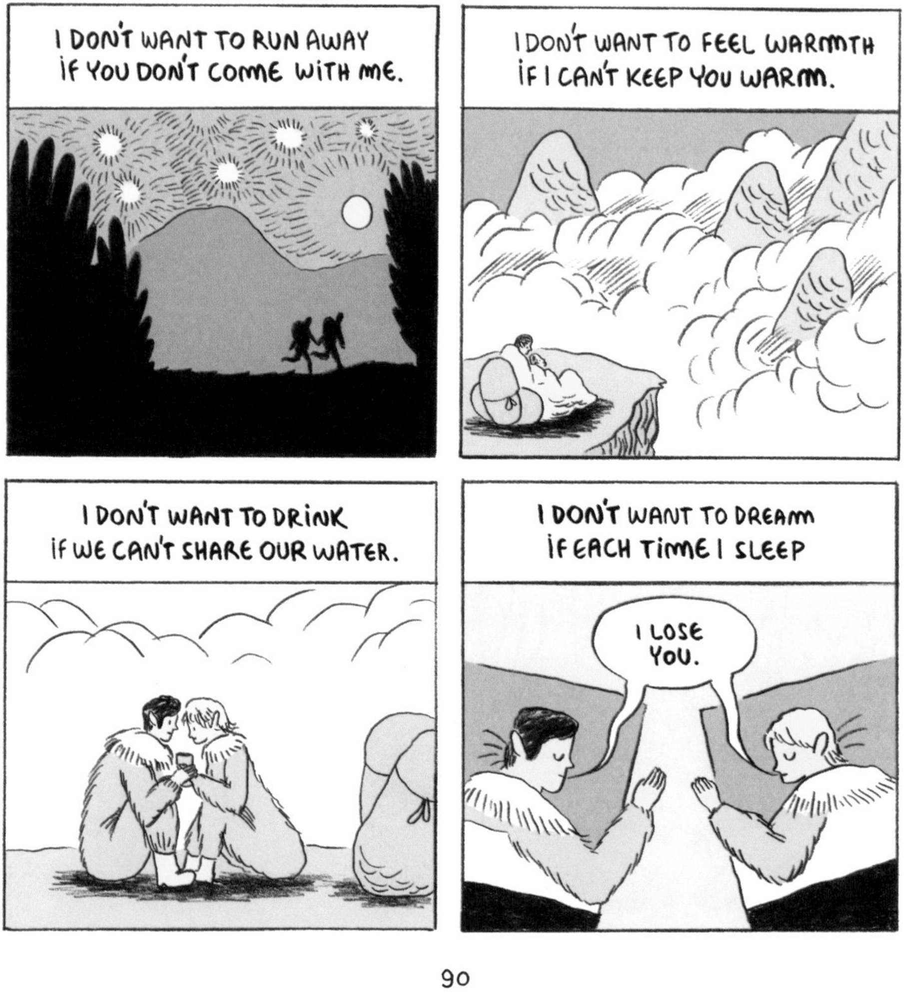
I DON'T WANT TO RUN AWAY IF YOU DON'T COME WITH ME.
I DON'T WANT TO FEEL WARMTH IF I CAN'T KEEP YOU WARM.
I DON'T WANT TO DRINK IF WE CAN'T SHARE OUR WATER.
I DON'T WANT TO DREAM IF EACH TIME I SLEEP
I LOSE YOU.

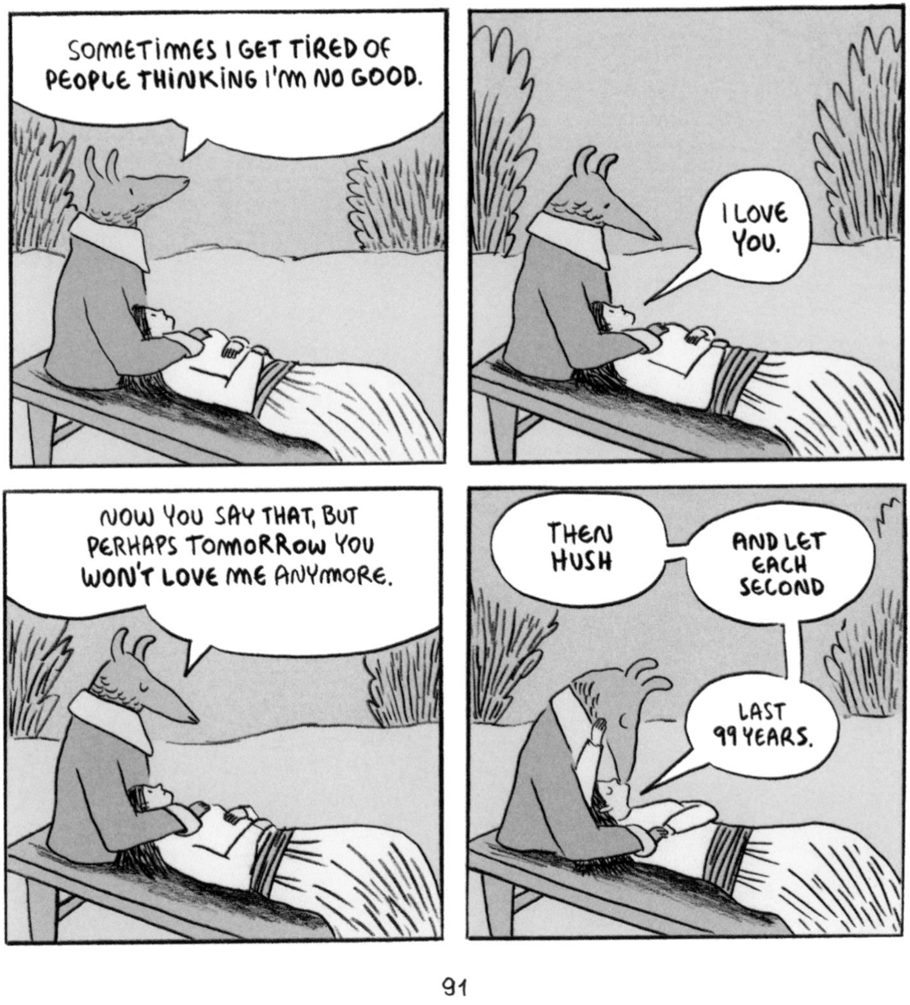
SOMETIMES I GET TIRED OF PEOPLE THINKING I'M NO GOOD.
I LOVE YOU.
NOW YOU SAY THAT, BUT PERHAPS TOMORROW YOU WON'T LOVE ME ANYMORE.
THEN HUSH
AND LET EACH SECOND
LAST 99 YEARS.

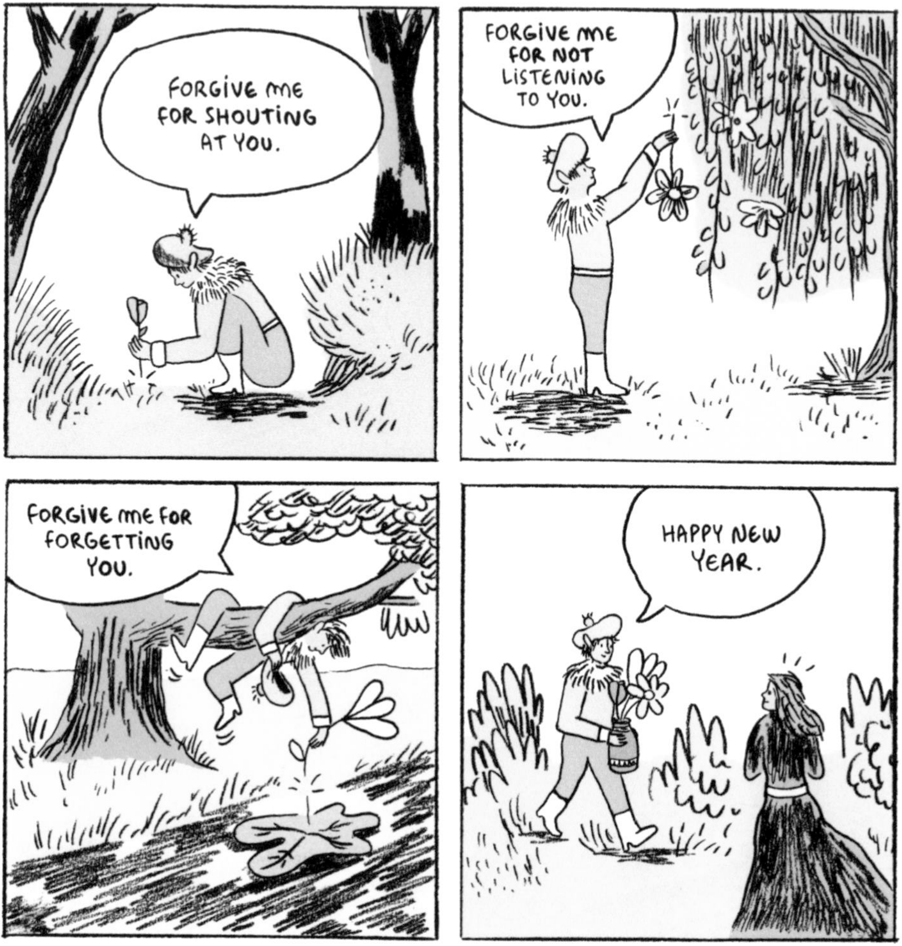
FORGIVE ME FOR SHOUTING AT YOU.
FORGIVE ME FOR NOT LISTENING TO YOU.
FORGIVE ME FOR FORGETTING YOU.
HAPPY NEW YEAR.

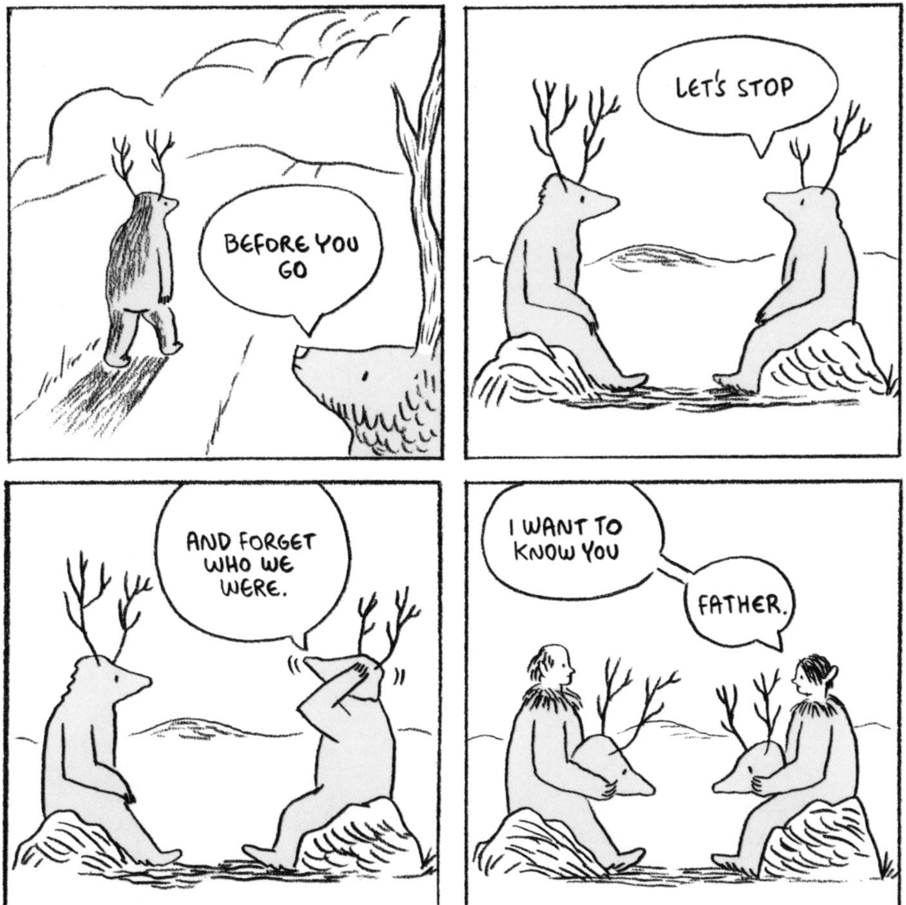
BEFORE YOU GO
LET'S STOP
AND FORGET WHO WE WERE.
I WANT TO KNOW YOU
FATHER.

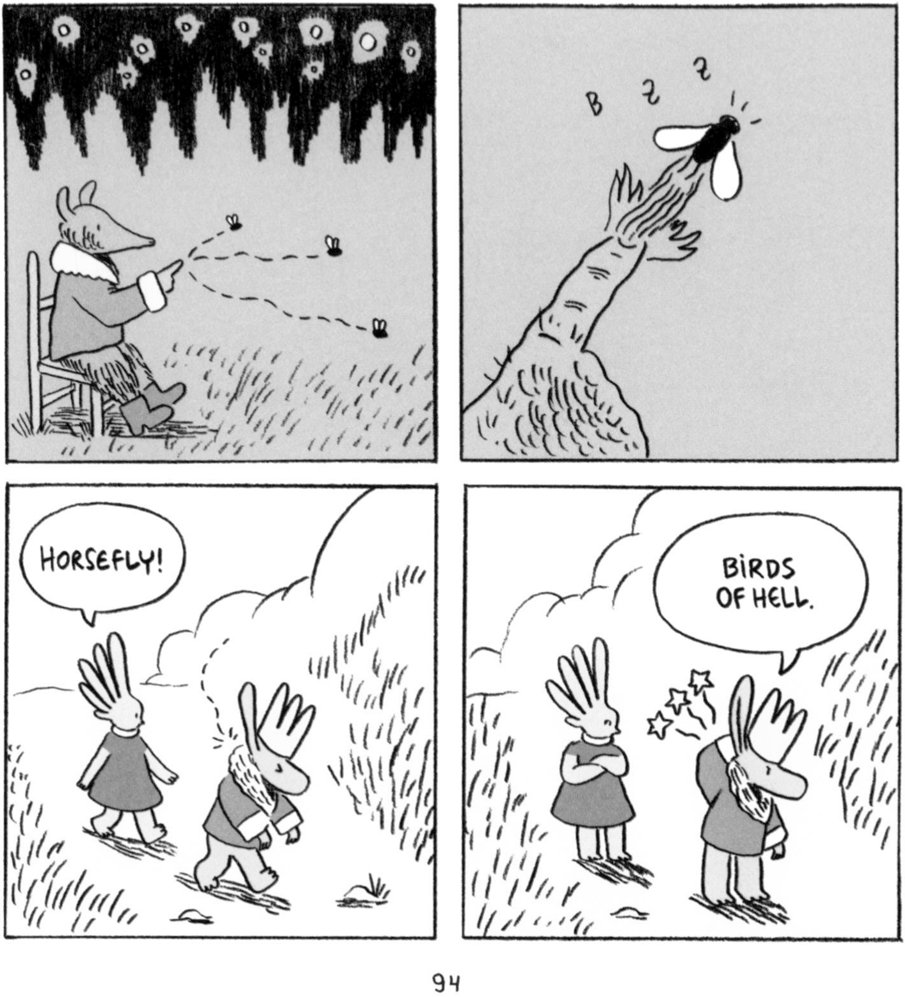
B Z Z
HORSEFLY!
BIRDS OF HELL.

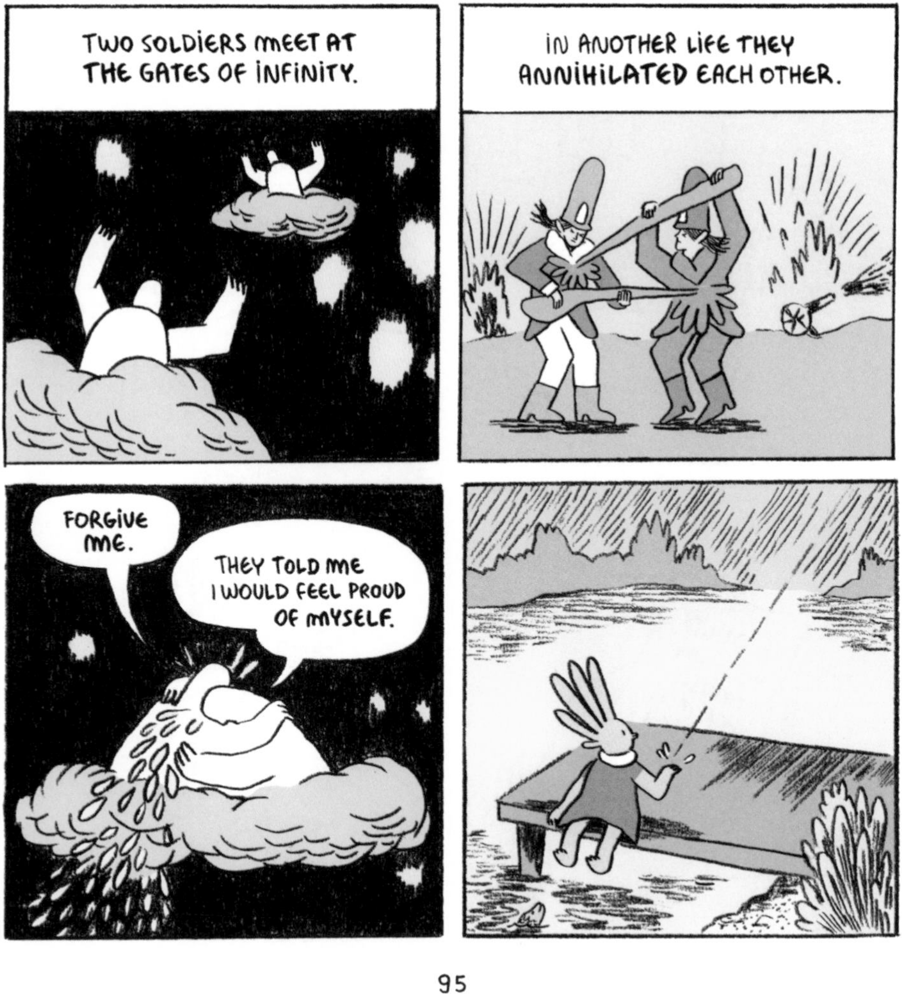
TWO SOLDIERS MEET AT THE GATES OF INFINITY.
IN ANOTHER LIFE THEY ANNIHILATED EACH OTHER.
FORGIVE ME.
THEY TOLD ME I WOULD FEEL PROUD OF MYSELF.

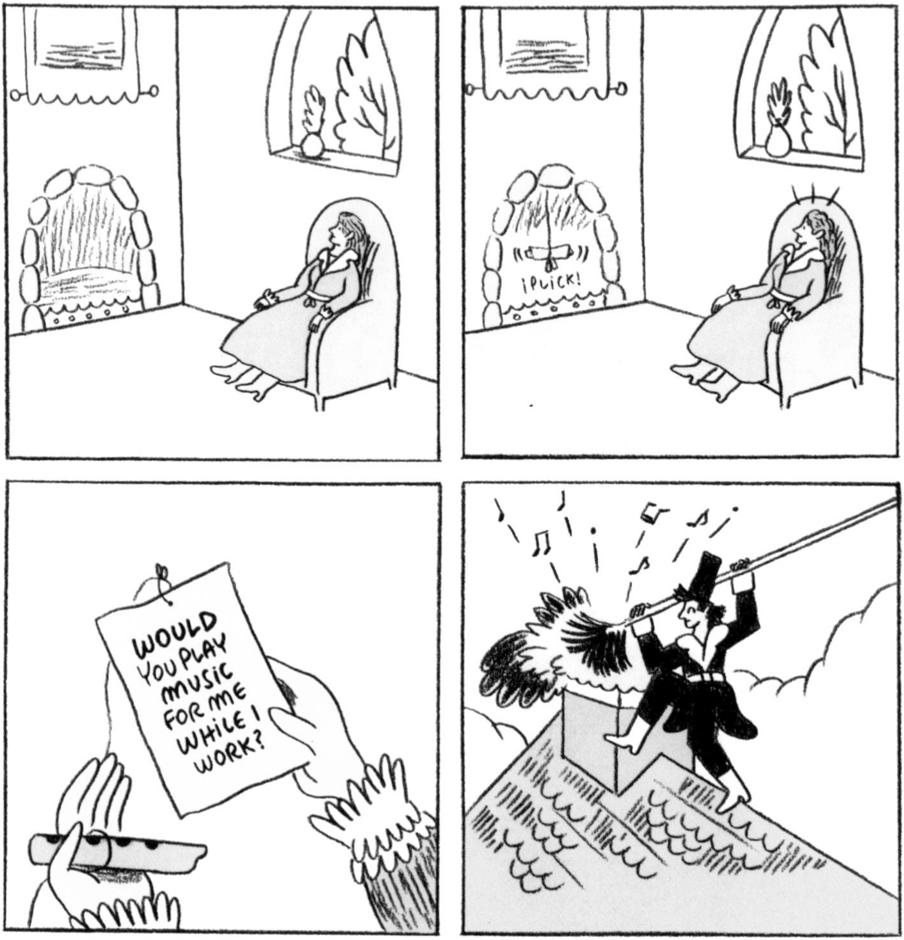
¡PLICK!
WOULD YOU PLAY MUSIC FOR ME WHILE I WORK?

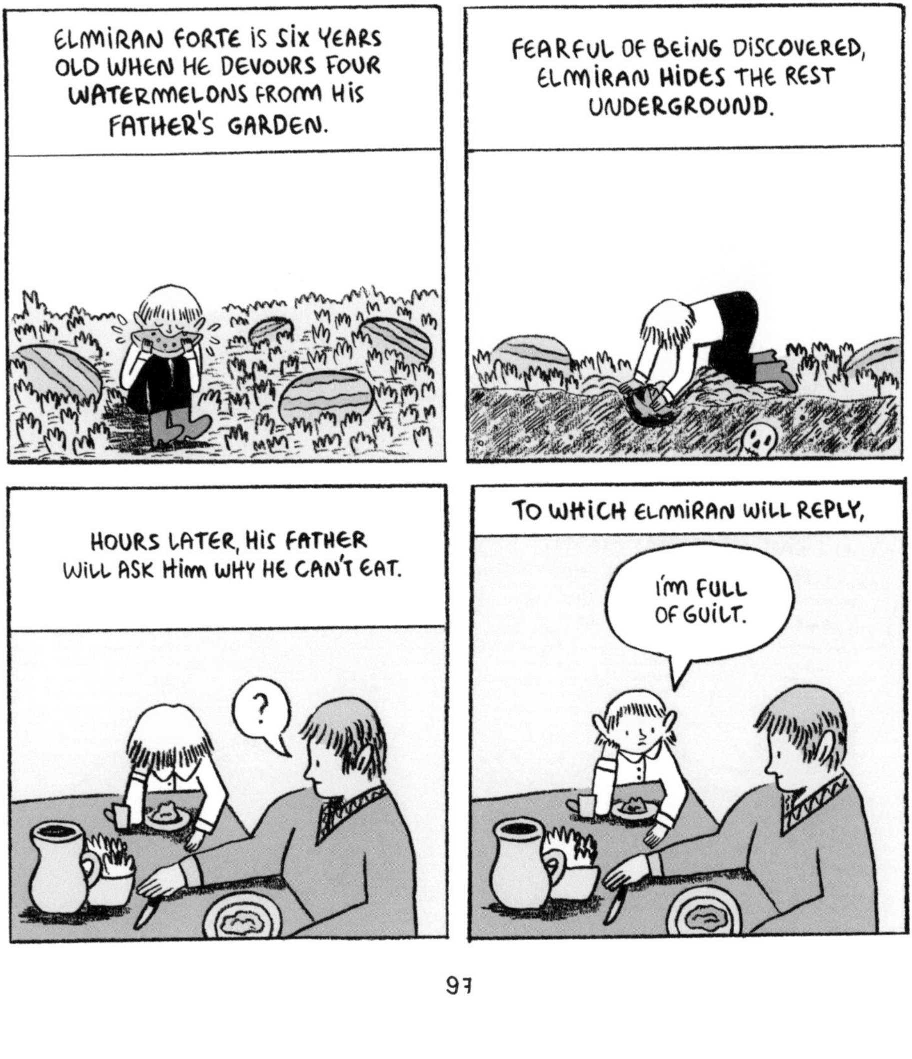
ELMIRAN FORTE IS SIX YEARS OLD WHEN HE DEVOURS FOUR WATERMELONS FROM HIS FATHER'S GARDEN.
FEARFUL OF BEING DISCOVERED, ELMIRAN HIDES THE REST UNDERGROUND.
HOURS LATER, HIS FATHER WILL ASK HIM WHY HE CAN'T EAT.
?
TO WHICH ELMIRAN WILL REPLY,
I'M FULL OF GUILT.

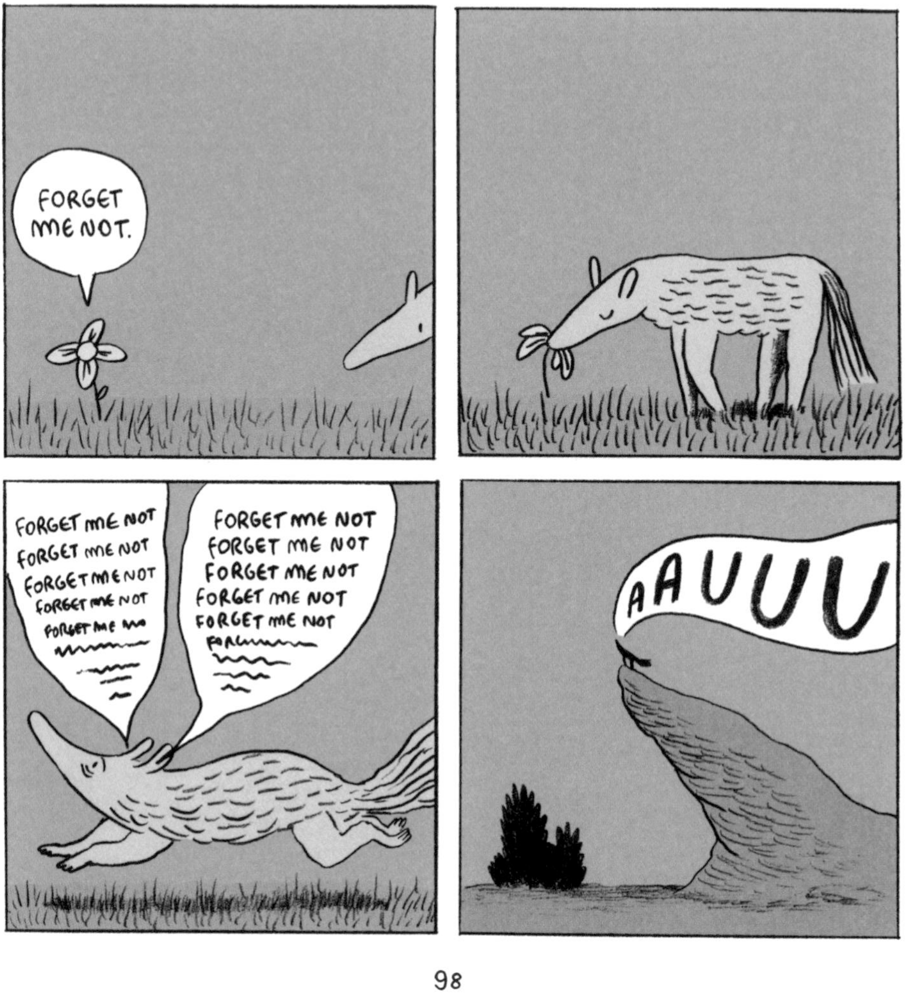
FORGET ME NOT.
FORGET ME NOT
FORGET ME NOT
FORGET ME NOT
FORGET ME NOT
FORGET ME NOT
FORGET ME NOT
FORGET ME NOT
FORGET ME NOT
FORGET ME NOT
FORGET ME NOT
AAUUU

IN YOUR BELLYBUTTON, MY FINGER
TWIRLS LIKE A SINKING WHIRLWIND,

UNTIL IT REACHES THE BOTTOM,

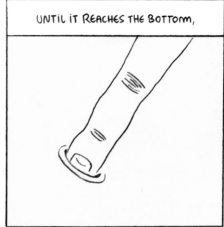

WHERE, FOR AN INSTANT, IT MEETS
A CONTINUATION OF MY LIFE.

DID
YOU FEEL IT?

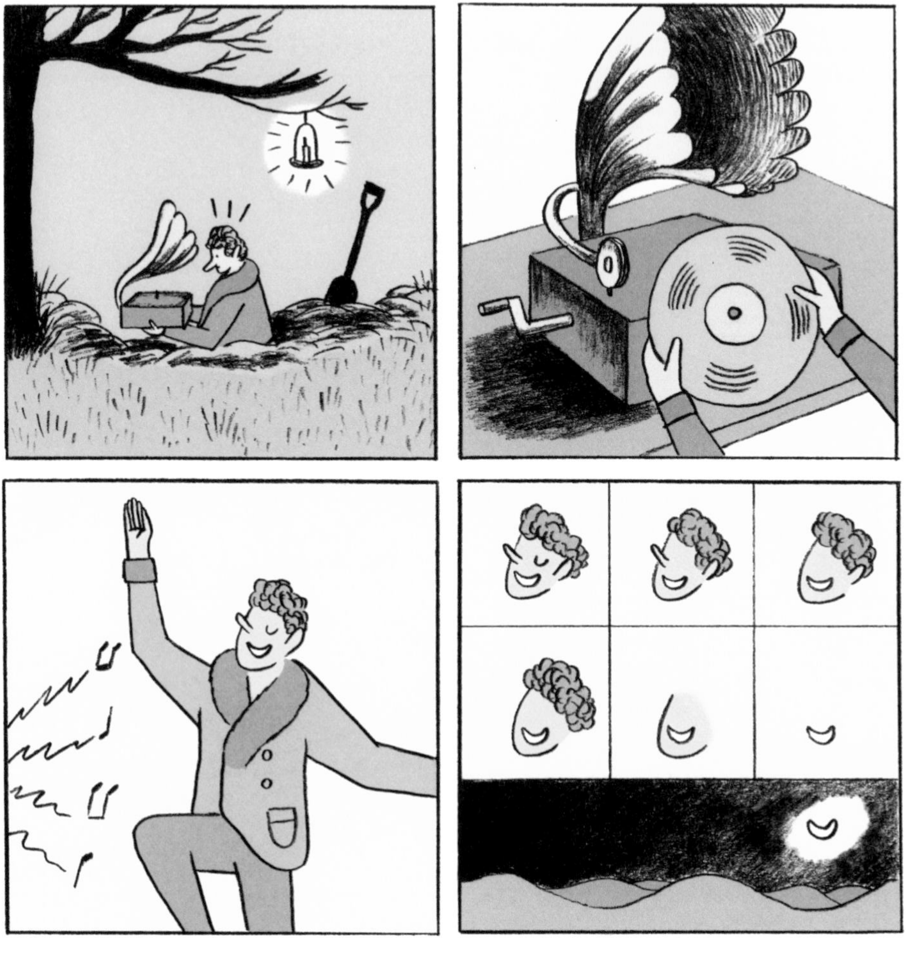

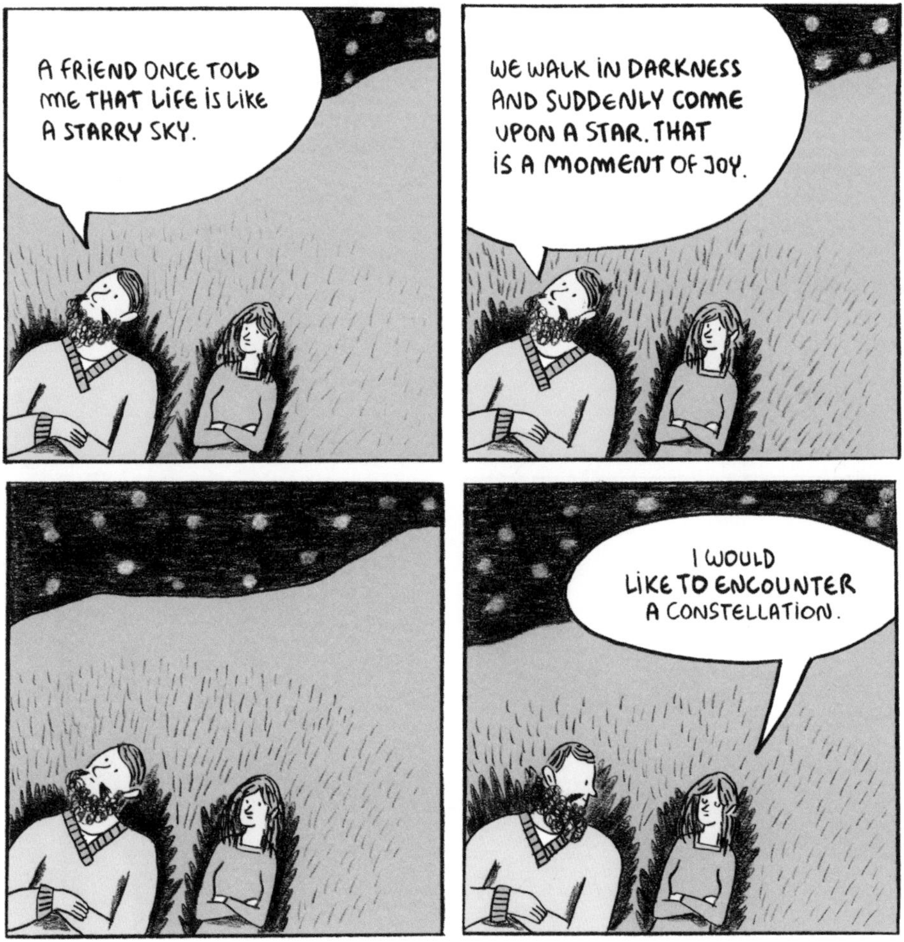
A FRIEND ONCE TOLD ME THAT LIFE IS LIKE A STARRY SKY.
WE WALK IN DARKNESS AND SUDDENLY COME UPON A STAR. THAT IS A MOMENT OF JOY.
I WOULD LIKE TO ENCOUNTER A CONSTELLATION.

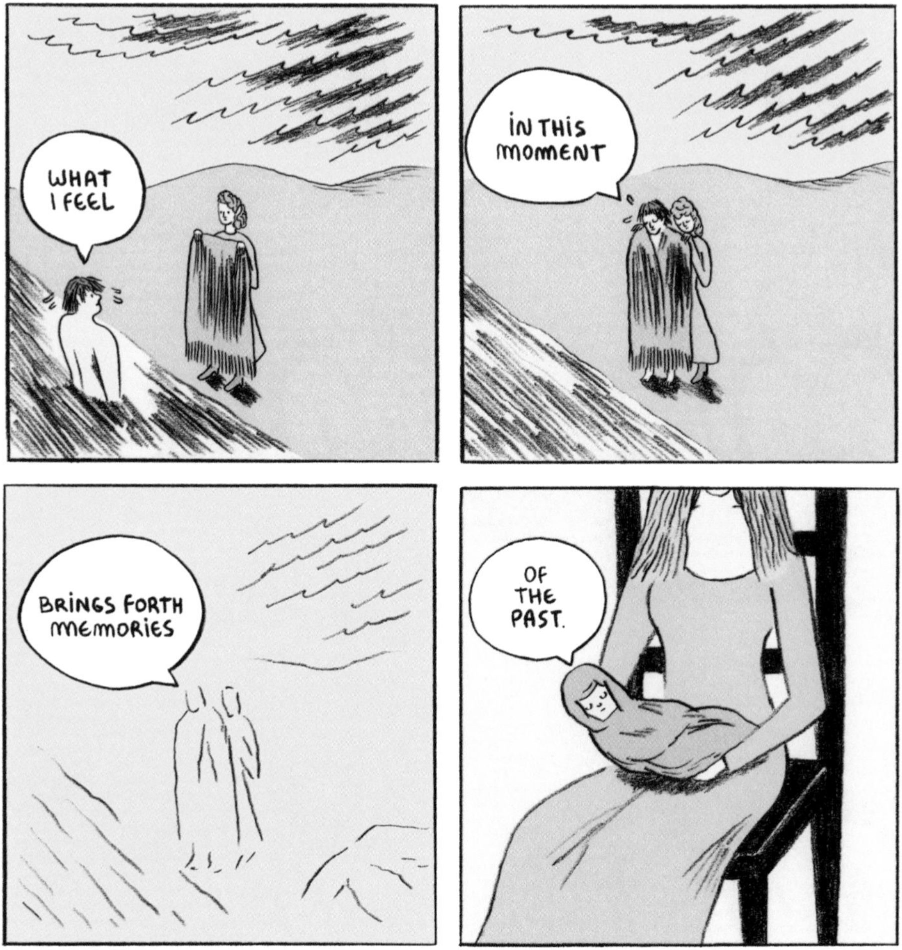
WHAT I FEEL
IN THIS MOMENT
BRINGS FORTH MEMORIES
OF THE PAST.

THEY DANCED AT NIGHTFALL

UNTIL A WORD SPRUNG FROM THE EARTH

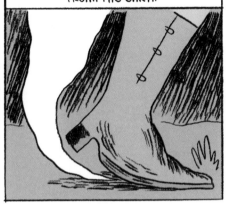

WHICH THEY CHOSE TO IGNORE FOR THE REST OF THE EVENING.

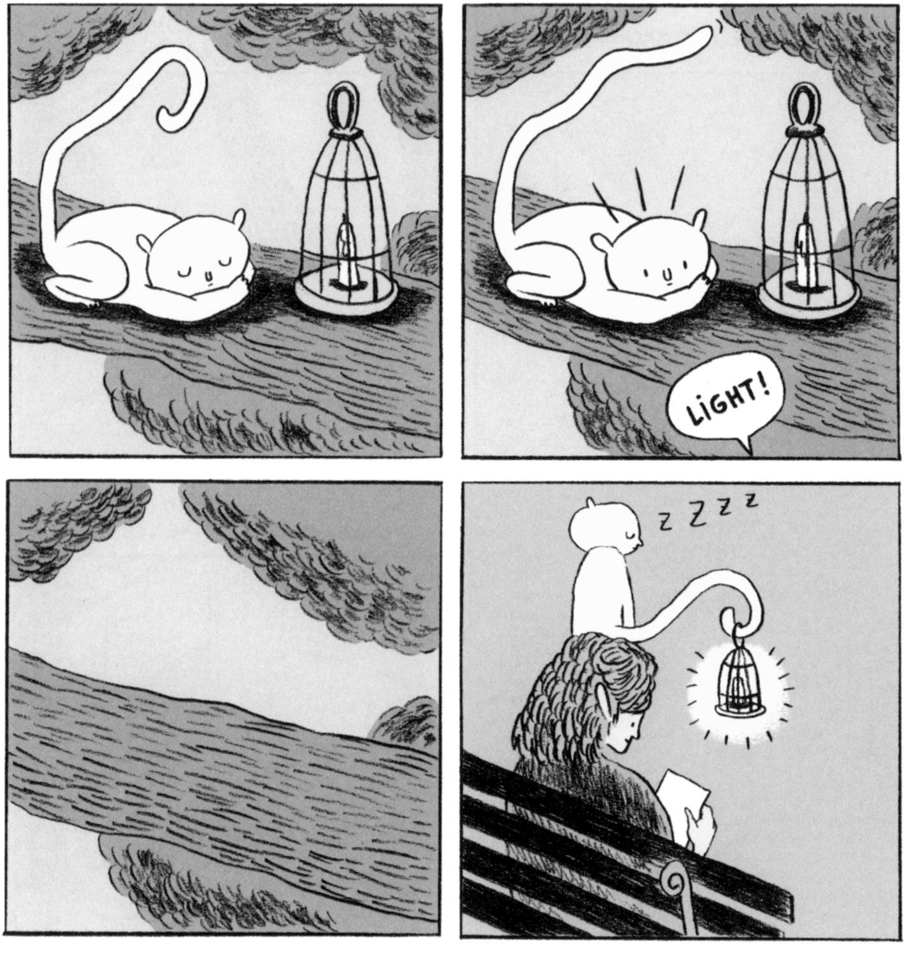
LIGHT!
Z Z Z Z

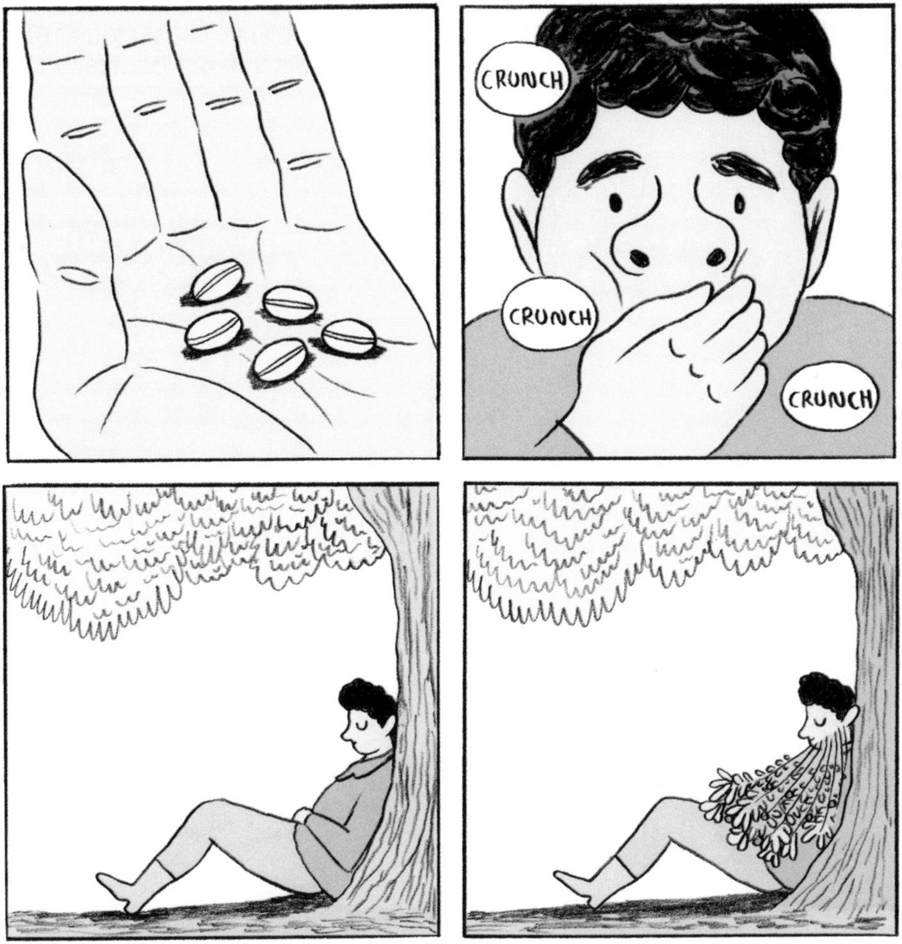
CRUNCH
CRUNCH
CRUNCH

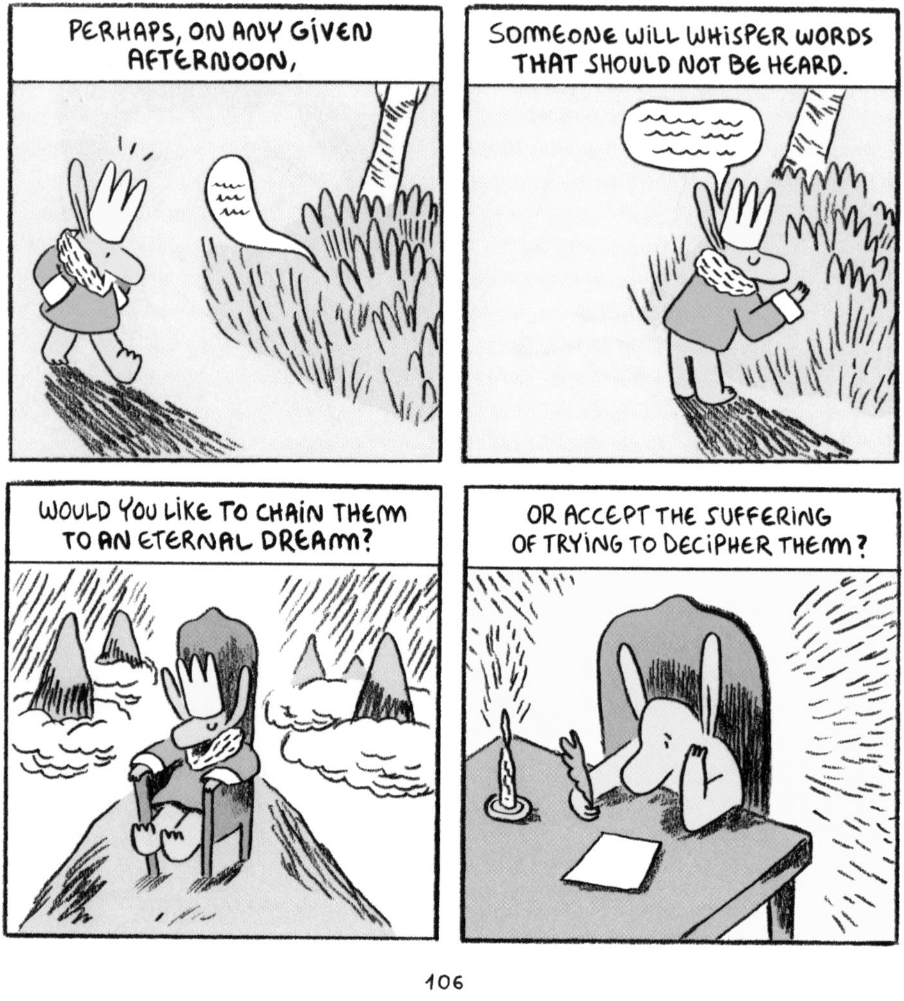
PERHAPS, ON ANY GIVEN AFTERNOON,
SOMEONE WILL WHISPER WORDS THAT SHOULD NOT BE HEARD.
WOULD YOU LIKE TO CHAIN THEM TO AN ETERNAL DREAM?
OR ACCEPT THE SUFFERING OF TRYING TO DECIPHER THEM?

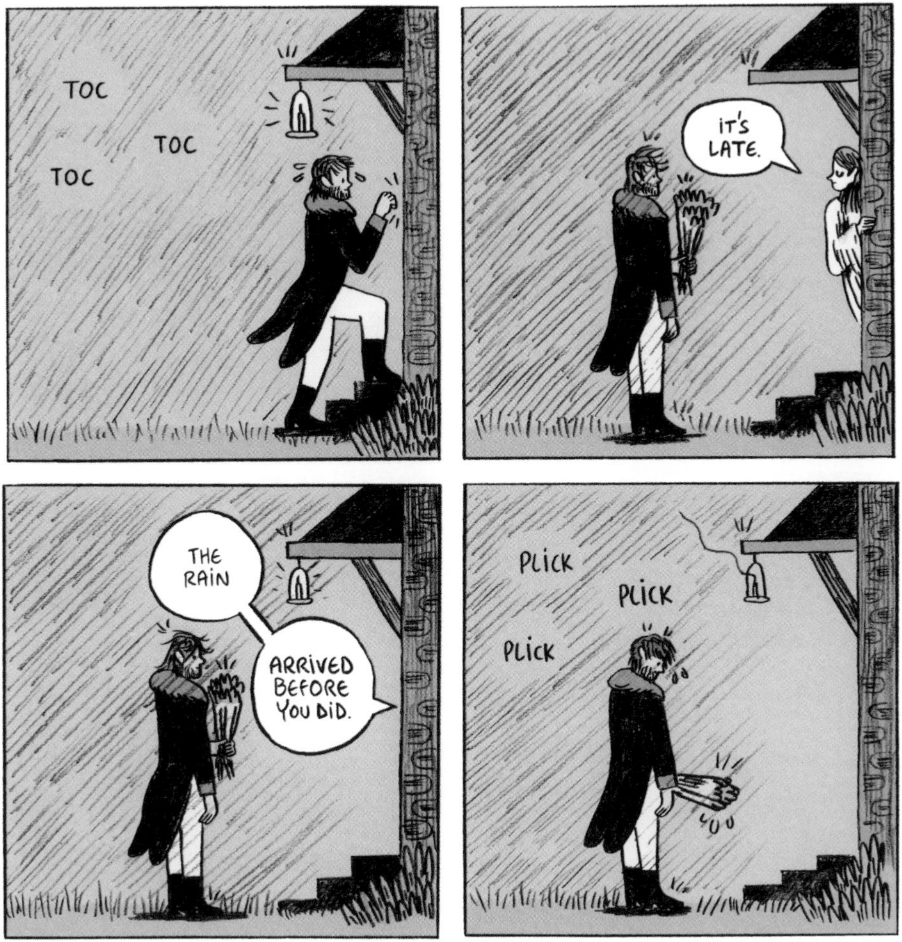
TOC
TOC
TOC
IT'S LATE.
THE RAIN
ARRIVED BEFORE YOU DID.
PLICK
PLICK
PLICK

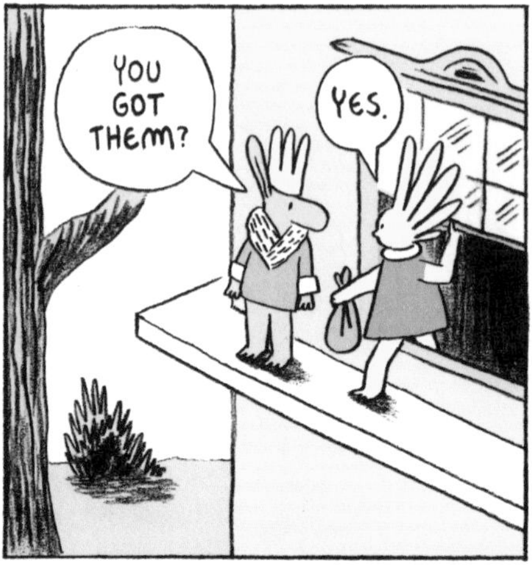
YOU GOT THEM?
YES.

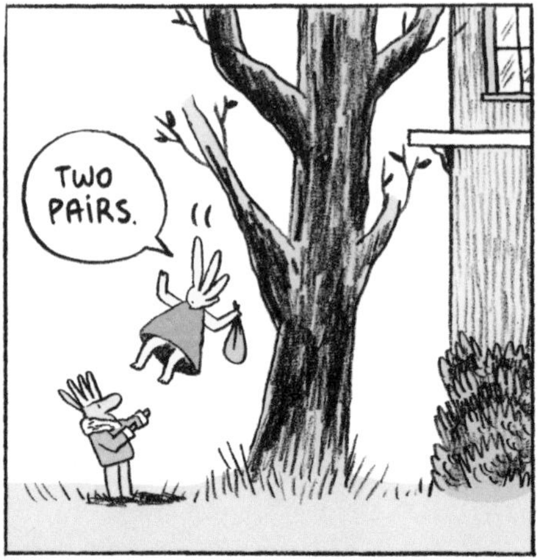
TWO PAIRS.

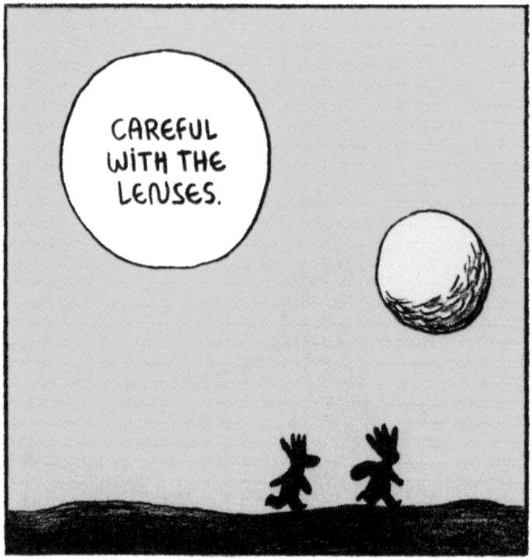
CAREFUL WITH THE LENSES.

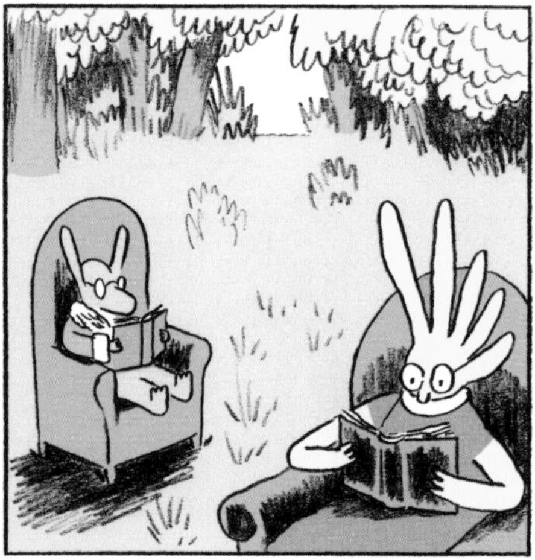

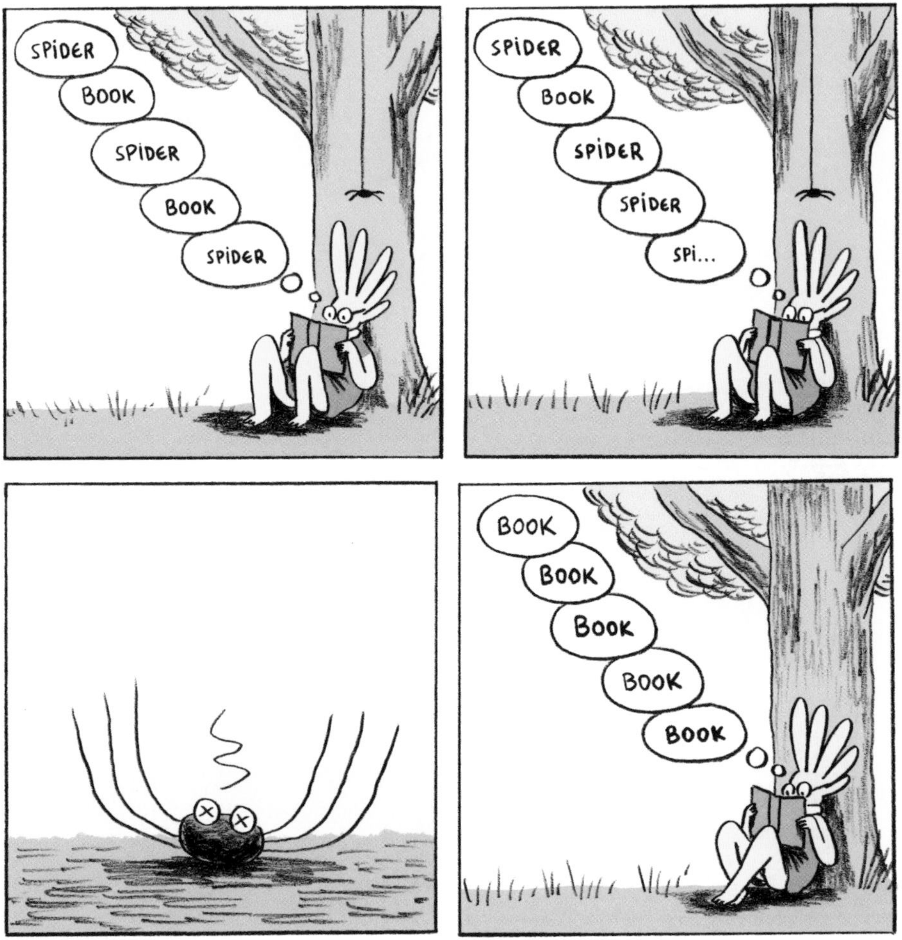
SPIDER
BOOK
SPIDER
BOOK
SPIDER
SPIDER
BOOK
SPIDER
SPIDER
SPI...
BOOK
BOOK
BOOK
BOOK
BOOK

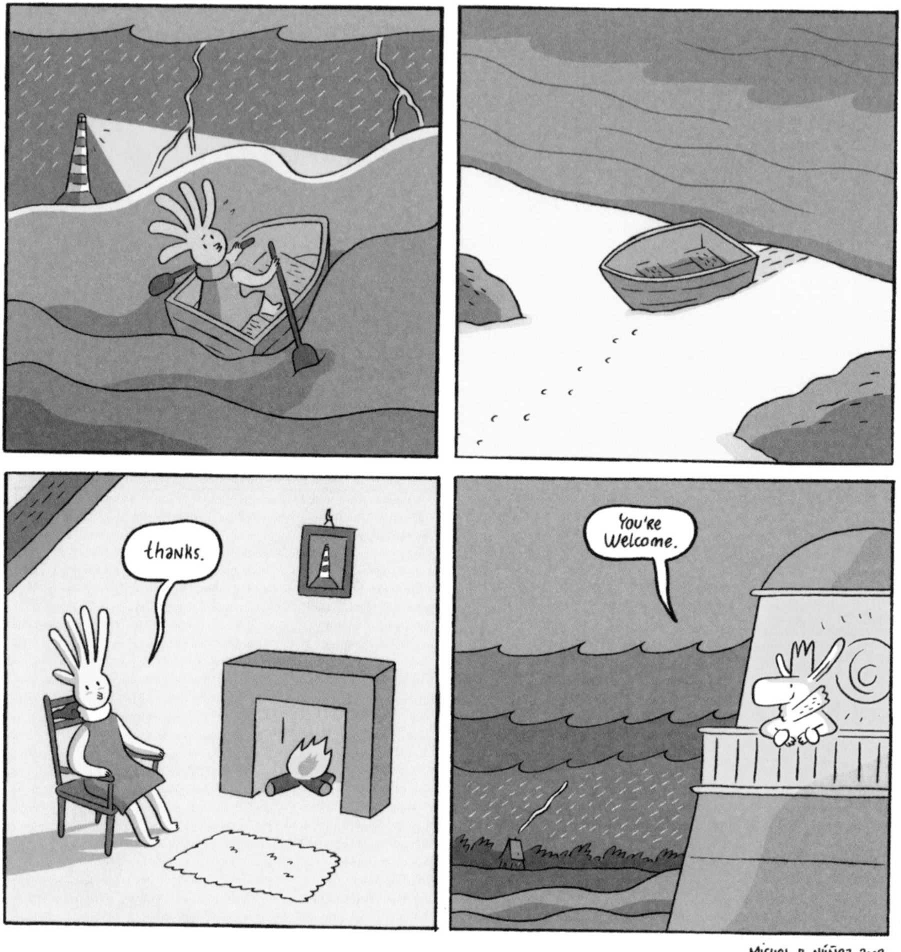
thanks.
You're Welcome.

MIGUEL B. NÚÑEZ 2009

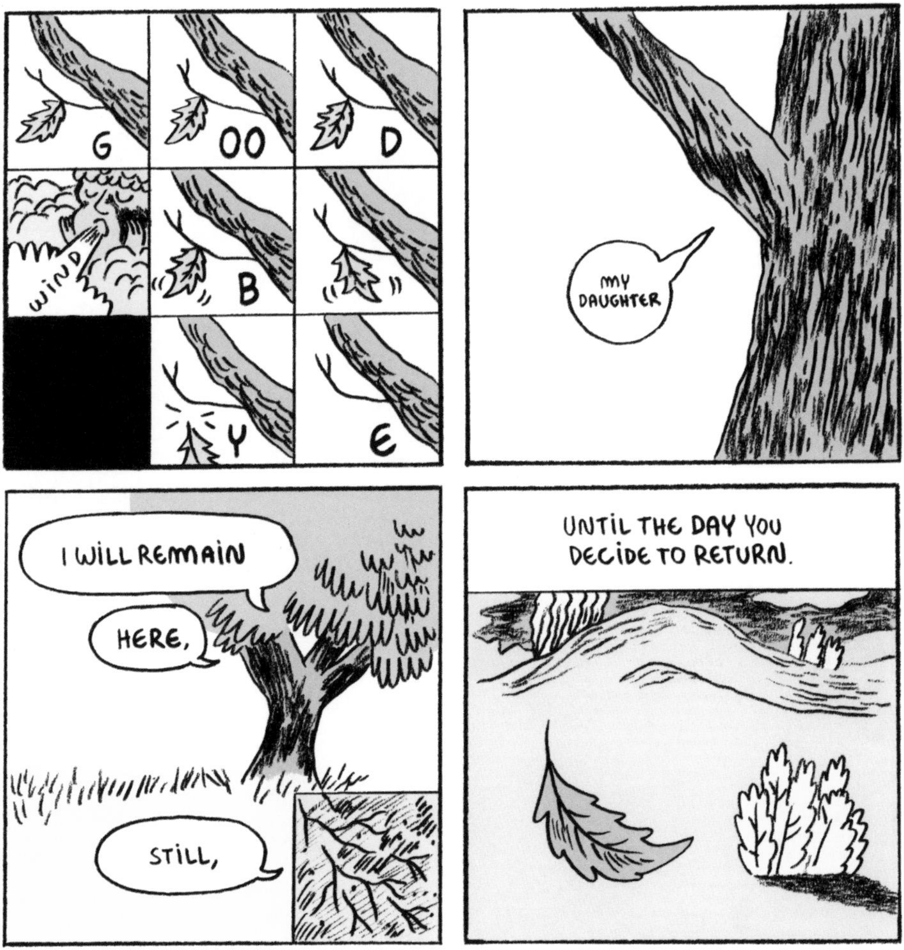
G
OO
D
WIND
B
Y
E
MY DAUGHTER
I WILL REMAIN
HERE,
STILL,
UNTIL THE DAY YOU DECIDE TO RETURN.

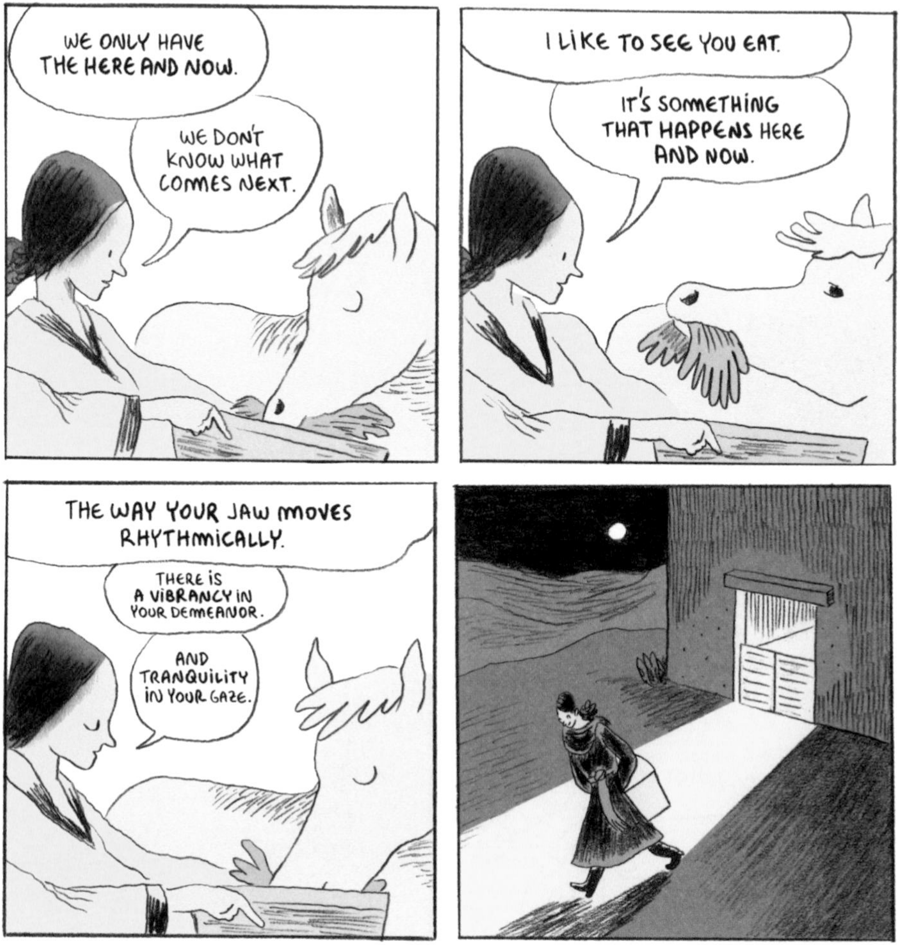
WE ONLY HAVE THE HERE AND NOW.
WE DON'T KNOW WHAT COMES NEXT.
I LIKE TO SEE YOU EAT.
IT'S SOMETHING THAT HAPPENS HERE AND NOW.
THE WAY YOUR JAW MOVES RHYTHMICALLY.
THERE IS A VIBRANCY IN YOUR DEMEANOR.
AND TRANQUILITY IN YOUR GAZE.

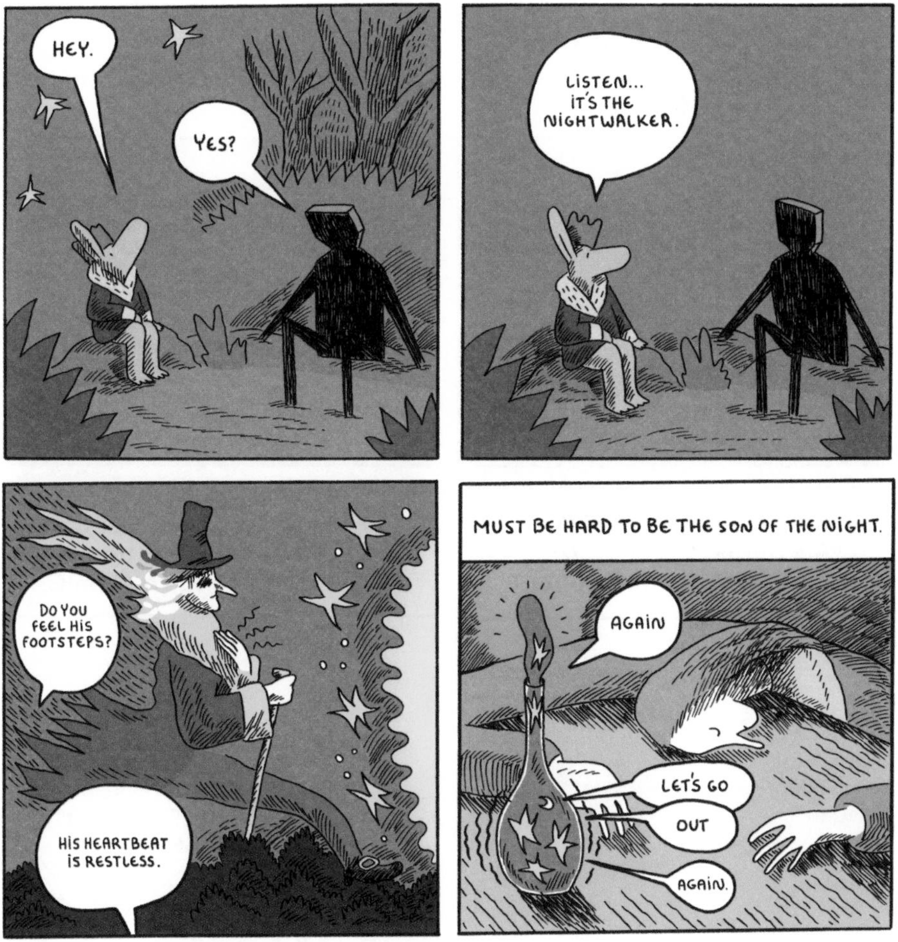
HEY.
YES?
LISTEN... IT'S THE NIGHTWALKER.
DO YOU FEEL HIS FOOTSTEPS?
HIS HEARTBEAT IS RESTLESS.
MUST BE HARD TO BE THE SON OF THE NIGHT.
AGAIN
LET'S GO
OUT
AGAIN.

THIS I GIVE YOU: MAN, FOR YOU TO MOLD AND DEFINE...

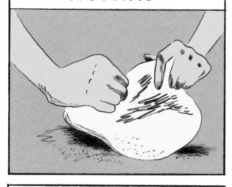

BREATHE LIFE INTO HIM.

AND WHAT DO I DO IF THE PAINT STARTS TO PEEL OFF... IF HE ENCOUNTERS DOUBT?

THEN YOU HAVE TO MEET UP WITH HIM YOURSELF, WOMAN. NEVER LEAVE HIM ALONE.

COULD YOU SHOW ME THE WAY TO THE NEXT PORT?

OF COURSE, MISS.

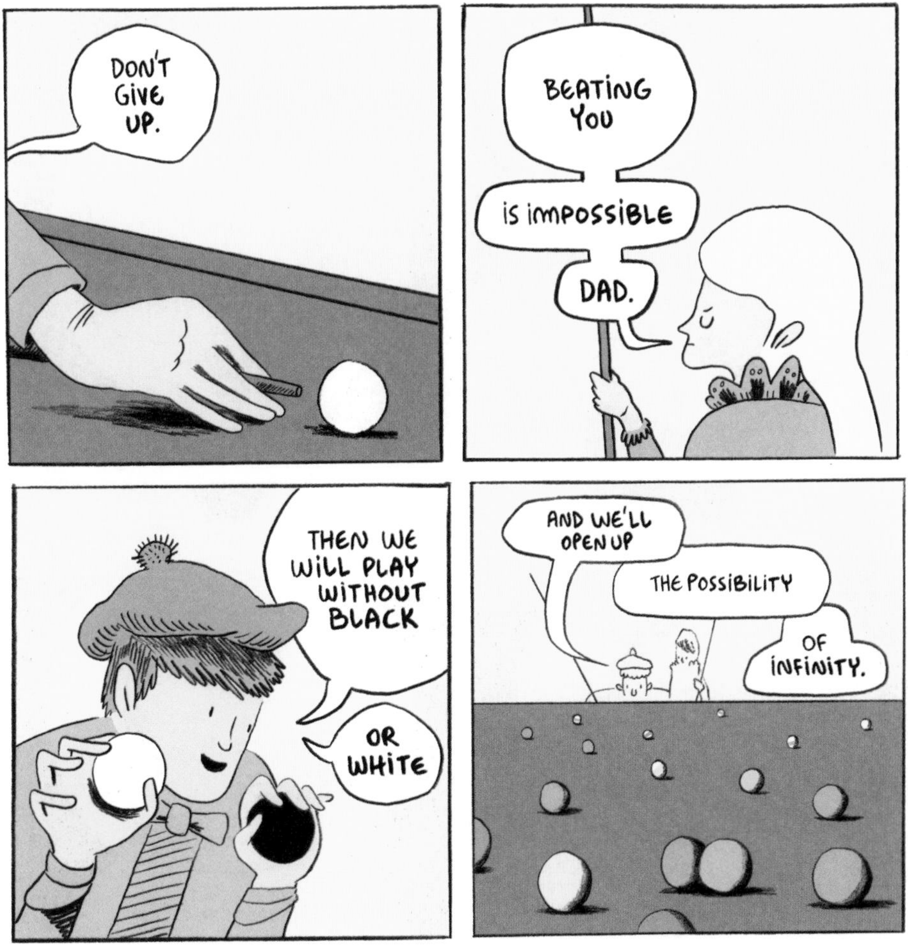
DON'T GIVE UP.
BEATING YOU
IS IMPOSSIBLE
DAD.
THEN WE WILL PLAY WITHOUT BLACK
OR WHITE
AND WE'LL OPEN UP
THE POSSIBILITY
OF INFINITY.

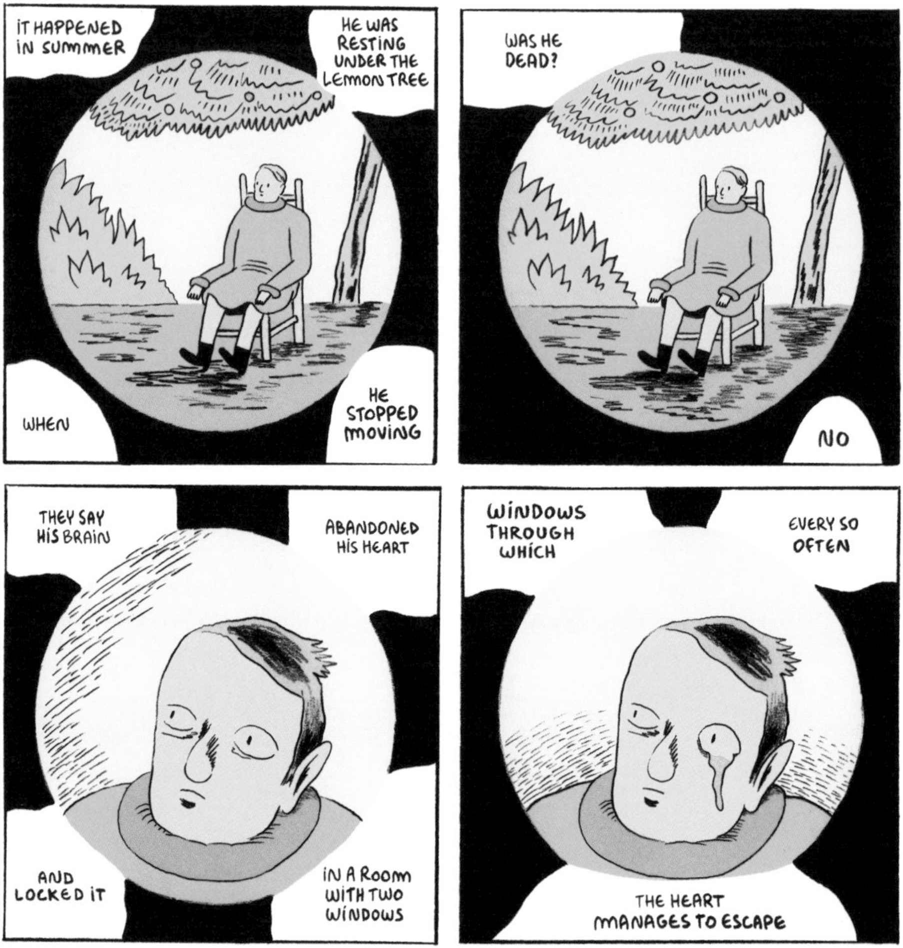
IT HAPPENED IN SUMMER
HE WAS RESTING UNDER THE LEMON TREE
WHEN
HE STOPPED MOVING
WAS HE DEAD?
NO
THEY SAY HIS BRAIN
ABANDONED HIS HEART
AND LOCKED IT
IN A ROOM WITH TWO WINDOWS
WINDOWS THROUGH WHICH
EVERY SO OFTEN
THE HEART MANAGES TO ESCAPE

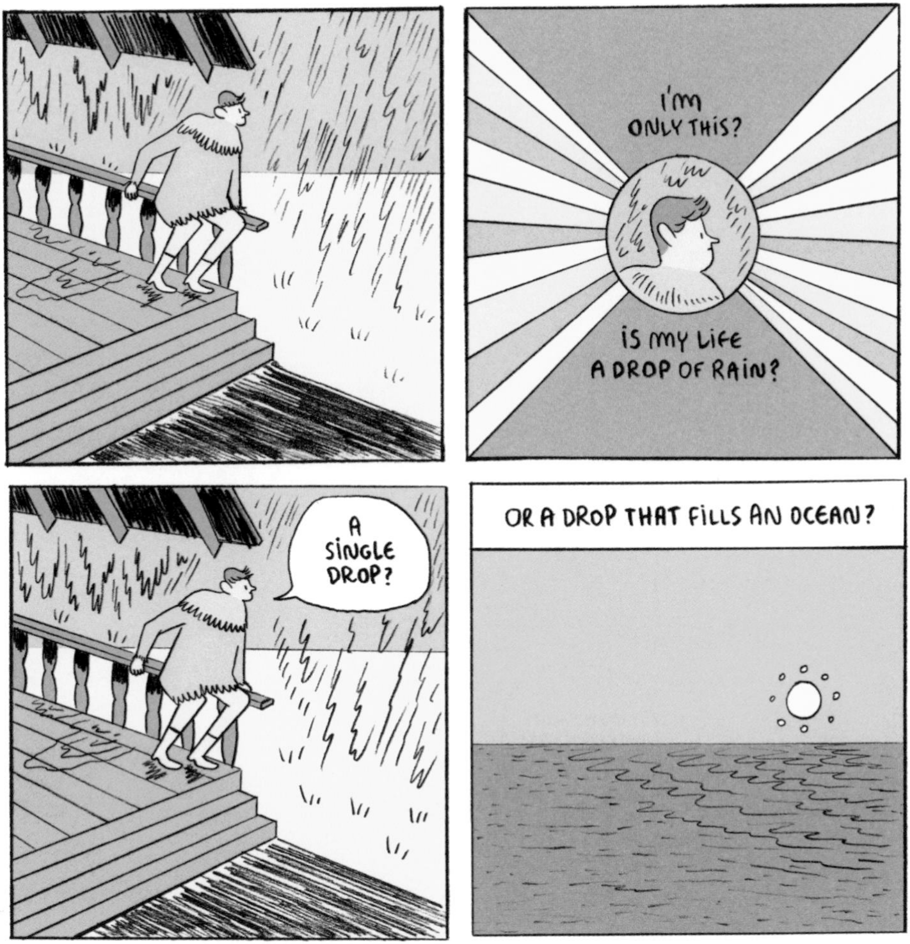
I'M ONLY THIS?
IS MY LIFE A DROP OF RAIN?
A SINGLE DROP?
OR A DROP THAT FILLS AN OCEAN?

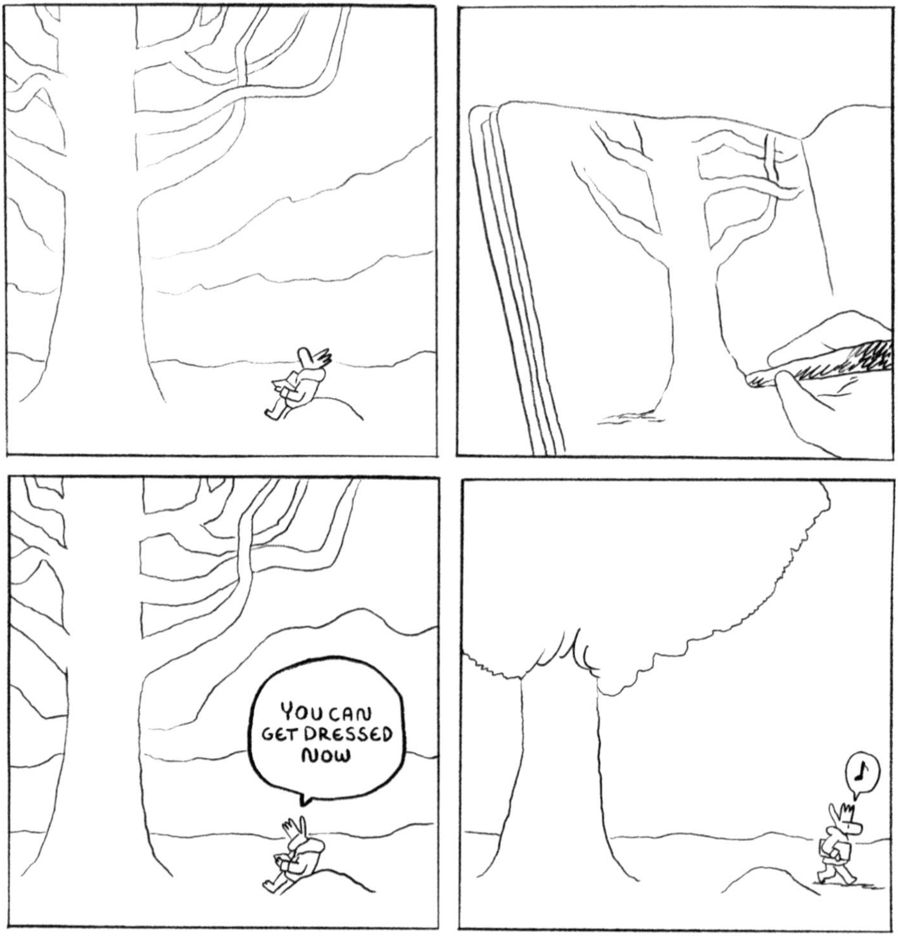
YOU CAN GET DRESSED NOW

PABLO HOLMBERG (KIOSKERMAN) WAS BORN IN BUENOS AIRES, ARGENTINA, IN 1979.
HE HAS BEEN DRAWING COMICS SINCE 2004, WHEN HE STARTED SERIALIZING
HIS STRIPS ON HIS WEBSITE: WWW.KIOSKERMAN.COM